Dear Love Life

Efficient Dating

in the

Technology Era

Sylvester McNutt III

Fourth Edition
September 2016

ISBN: 1518659551
ISBN-13: 978-1518659553

The names in all of these stories, poems, and anecdotes have been changed to protect the identities of any person(s) real, exaggerated, or made up. *Dear Love Life: Efficient Dating in the Technology Era* and Sylvester McNutt III are not replacements for professional help, counseling, or guidance. If you need a psychological evaluation or counseling, then you must seek the proper help. This book is written from the perspective and opinion of the creator, and he reserves the right, at any moment, to change his perception of anything presented. The author, the publisher, or person responsible for delivering you this text is not liable for any undesirable outcome.

Welcome to
Dear Love Life:
Efficient Dating in the
Technology Era
by Sylvester McNutt III

www.sylvestermcnutt.com

Cover and illustrations by Topher Kirby
www.topherwrites.com

Media inquiries, wholesale purchases, or any other needs, please contact the author directly at **slymcnutt@gmail.com**. I'd love to connect with you on social media. Here are the four sites that I use.

Instagram—www.instagram.com/sylvestermcnutt

YouTube—**www.youtube.com/slymcnutt**

Snapchat—@SylvesterMcNutt

Facebook— Sylvester McNutt III

Table of Contents

Love-Awakening Transformation

Epiphany, light bulbs, bright ideas, and aha moments saturate and excite our daily human lives as we have strokes of human genius throughout it. Some people say there is good that can come out of every situation. It's hard to believe that when you're going through hell on earth. Sometimes we wake up our states of suffering because we find good books, beautiful sunsets, or great shows on Netflix. Then, on the other end, there are people who have the innate ability to learn, grow, and prosper without negative events and thoughts. Some humans just grow out of observation, environment, and training; others need trauma, negativity, and the short end of the stick. Everyone goes a different direction, but either way there has to be some feeling of a raised consciousness. A feeling that things aren't right. A feeling like life as we know it could be better. Once a person arrives at this feeling, especially toward his or her dating situation, this person has started a consciousness evolution inside of his or her heart and spirit.

It only takes one heartbreak, one broken promise, or one loved one to desert you like you meant nothing. It only takes one moment of sleeping alone and just craving and longing for a soul, but not any soul, the one who understands you. You've meditated, prayed, and overobsessed what this other person may be like. It only takes for you to watch one show, to read one book, or to see one couple who inspires you to want love. Your biology tells you to seek love and acceptance from one or many, depending on you. *Many* can mean friends, family, and a loved one. *Many* can also suffice as one; everyone is different. No matter what your *Dear Love Life* reads like, please understand that this book revolves around one premise: love needs people to use efficient skills and behaviors to alleviate pain, to instill happiness, and to make it last past the cupcake stage.

Your awareness is constantly being realized or ignored, depending on you. Take a realistic inventory of where you are, what you have, what you bring to the table, what you could be doing wrong, what you could do more of. It's imperative that you introspect, objectively, everything you are and are not. You have to audit yourself. No matter what, you'll be able to feel a shift or change in you. This is your *love awakening*—it may feel like something has changed or is changing; you may start critiquing and fighting your old habits or viewpoints on life. You may undergo an increased connection to your intuition, the physical world around you, or the knowledge you acquire. I'm willing to bet my next meal that if you're reading this book, you're in a transformative transition stage that has no start or end, but it exists right now as a phase of shifting.

When you experience your love awakening, do not fear or resist it. You have to experience it fully, without resistance and negativity from your inner thoughts. You may experience this while you're currently in a committed relationship. It's not a sign to leave and abandon the relationship. It's a sign that you may be responsible for raising the vibrations in the relationship; you may be the one. Whatever *the one* means to you, understand that at some point, we all should feel like we are the one. Not from a self-serving, ego way, no. From a self-powering, self-accountability, and agent-of-change type of way. It's for your actions, thoughts, and awareness. This shift is happening deep inside of you. Let it. This is your consciousness preparing for you to vibrate higher as a being of love.

Love, dating, communication, and other variables of human interactions that calculate the total makeup of a relationship vary based on desire, skill, and perception.

Throughout time, gurus, poets, and scholars have tried to explain dating from perspectives of men and women. The truth is that there isn't one blanket method that works for every human being or every relationship. This is why it is imperative that we amass an uncanny amalgamation of skills, awareness, and understanding that will keep our chances of success high and consistent. We have many problems, conflict, and confusion going around when it comes to love, dating, and relationships because of a lack of awareness, training, and realistic gatherings. Our schools do not raise us to learn love, efficient dating, and proactive learning in relationships. Love and romance are not represented in mass media from an introspective, learning perspective. I know something about you, and I'm willing to bet my next meal on it: You care about love. You care about your relationships. You want to improve your relationships with your friends, your coworkers, and yourself. I guarantee you're the type of person who loves to give, who loves to feel alive, and you're first in line to always take care of other people.

You may have been raised the exact same way that your brother or sister was raised, but you'll see a great deal of contrast in your dating lanes and outcomes.

Humans across time have shown that there literally are no rules to dating successfully. The term *success* has taken off over the last hundred years as it has become the driving force behind the industrial revolution, economic booms, and global trade of goods and services. Today, we must look at, introspect, and understand a massive array of skills and outcomes in order to make us efficient and successful in matters of our *Dear Love Life*. It's our inalienable right to desire love; we want to feel as if we belong to a group of loving or at least accepting individuals, from our perspective. In many cases we live with strife and conflict, anger and distrust, guile and ego as they permeate our ability to love efficiently. The text has one clear purpose, and that is to expand your consciousness around the concept that dating isn't solely about the fleeting emotions that enrage and spark us to give hugs that we wish would never go away. The purpose of the text is to challenge your consciousness, to push your current realm of thought, and to create a more efficient mind. No, this text will not offer illusory terms that only appease and feed your ego. The text here exists to give you what you need, what you crave—substance, authenticity. The text does not give you what you want to hear, only what you need, and as the curator, I promise I did not set out to appease anyone—meaning you may stumble upon thoughts, situations, and wording that are uncomfortable and dangerous. I want you to stay there. The comfort zone is most likely keeping you away from the evolution that you so desperately crave.

Your mission is to expand your consciousness via introspection and awareness. Indulging in too much information in one sitting can cause a sensory overload. It's best if you absorb while taking notes and reflecting on the text. I encourage you to write, to speak, and to record yourself throughout the text. I do not come to you with a goal of feeding you information with the purpose of you accepting it as it is. No. I am not that type of writer or person. This text is a skeleton of what your soul needs. It's up to you to give it flesh. Question everything, not just here, but forever.

Someone with no dating skills but dating desire will gain a blueprint to create consistent efficiency from his or her introspection of the text. My second underlying goal is to help the observer, you, to tap into a level of consciousness and self-power that you never knew existed. It's vital that you get ahead of the curve, be ahead of the wave, be the wave—you're not here to drown under the madness of uncertainty and unknowing. I overheard someone saying that the solution to dating is to teach men to be better. Claims like this are laughable, egregious, and shortsighted. Dating, love, and relationships can never be the fault of one gender, one person, or one event. You'll find that I will not allow you to be a victim throughout this text. We are here for accountability, growth, and purpose.

We are experiencing a consciousness shift in our generation and time period. This is the most important time period of our generation. Our generation is becoming weaker, ghostly, and unconscious day by day. We're allowing fictitious human behaviors, lifestyles, and vanity points to ruin our ability to be authentic and loving. Money, greed, and the concept of power is directing behaviors, cities, and people.

This isn't a "we are the world" or "save the children" type of text. No, it's much more important than that. *Dear Love Life* is an amalgamation of years of research, the deepest level of introspection, and psychology in order for us to become masters of our own love lanes.

Blanket statements are made across the world that hold weight, but they do not hold any substance or true direction, such as "Just love yourself" or "Do better." I love puny one-liners, but their only real purpose is to appease authors' egos once the phrases get reposted or accumulate enough likes online.

No, I reject that because we need more substance; we need depth, a depth so deep that it becomes black and overpowering like the deep-blue sea that loses its hue once we dive far enough to render our imagination useless. We need love not to be a catchphrase but to be a subject in school. I've written this book in a format that will allow a teacher, professor, or parent to present this as lesson plans. One should be able to get an advanced degree in love. There should be love breaks at work. If I can serve customers for eight to ten hours a day, where is my twenty-minute break to check in on my relationship? Stop it. The one-hour lunch break, if we're lucky, is for eating. We should be given breaks to check in on our relationships because nothing, and I mean nothing, operates without relationships. This idea is not farfetched. It just takes someone crazy enough like me to say that it should be the norm, and then you and your friends get behind it.

If we can make stupid people famous, if we can turn a blind eye to things like racism, sexism, and hate, then why can't we get behind an idea that is culture shifting? Just think about that. If you are a teacher, a business owner, or a manager, I challenge you to think of how you can give your students, employees, and assets time to love. As a student, a worker, or a businessperson, make time for this too. Even if it's just sending a quick e-mail or a short call to a loved one. Do not neglect love. Our mind-set today does not account for the most important part of our human functions. We take lunch breaks at work in order to nourish and hydrate our bodies, but we don't take love breaks? We have set schedules to work for corporations that get rich off of all of our collective efforts, but what about our schedules to love, to introspect, to reflect? Why aren't we being given time to explore the things that truly make us feel alive? These questions, this train of thought, this logic is the logic that is going to save our generation and spark a new paradigm shift. Some of us are ahead of the curve, some of us are leading it, and the rest of us are getting on the wave now.

After devouring this text and then purging your life of toxic behaviors, mind-sets, and people—if necessary—you'll no longer allow yourself to operate at a frequency level that doesn't serve you or your community. Through the text, I command you to grow, to proposer, and to become the leader in your organization.

Yes, the range of inspiration you will gain will vary based on how open you are to being shifted and transformed. You may feel as if you have everything you need because you've been married for fifteen years. You may be lost in the translation of stress or discourse. Or you may be reading this book because of the really eye-appealing cover art. No matter what your reason is for reading this book, trust me; trust yourself. I assure you that this text will spark something inside of you that will transform your *Dear Love Life*, now and forever.

This generation is in a bad place. The murder; the divorce rate; the police brutality; the terrorism; and the hate for race, gender, and class has now spread all over the world.

There are places where we can look up and say, "That's not fair" or "They're not being treated right." The language of this text is English, but once the messages are decoded, we'll see that this text contains a universal language that all countries, ethnic backgrounds, and diversities of individuals can understand—love.

Transformations in love literally change lives. Love is the most powerful drug on the planet, and it's your time to overdose on the taste. Many of the world's problems can be solved if we instill love throughout our dialogues and teachings. I have so much love inside of me that I have no desire to cause harm to any man. I do not want to see anyone in pain. I do not believe that pain, suffering, and negativity are necessary. I want everyone, even people who have unfavorable thoughts about me, to succeed and prosper. We as humans can heal and change the course of our collective direction.

I encourage you to share any and every page of the book on your social network account, with friends over group text messaging, and through any other forms of media. Take a picture of yourself reading and post it to your social media accounts; tell them that you're reading a book about love. I assure that you were led to these words because you deserve to be the most efficient lover possible. I beg you, the universe begs you, not to keep all of these secrets to yourself. It's imperative and vital to mankind that we spread this text on our *Dear Love Life* as we transform.

If I forget at the end to thank you, please allow me this moment to say something. I truly believe in the art of writing. I respect the art. I respect that in order to put a book together, ten thousand or more hours need to be exhausted in order to make the deepest impact on readers. I want to thank you because you were the reason I had sleepless nights. You are my purpose, as a human and as an artist. You and I have a relationship. I am the artist, and you are the observer. I want to thank you for this. I want you to know that I tried my absolute best to research, to rewrite, to create dialogue, to introspect so I could bring you the most impactful book of your life. I truly hope *Dear Love Life* touches a part of your soul and impacts your daily life in a positive way. Thank you for giving me a chance to share this with you.

Why I'm Writing You:
Dear Love Life

I've written to you before, in journal format, but those capsules of time contained a soul who was looking to grow in the lane of love and life. The writer at that time invited the observer into a path of self-love and the avenue of living in love after pain. Now it is a new day, and the conclusion of this series, the Dear Love series, is a unification of conscious thought and awareness.

I was asleep one day, and I had a dream; the dream told me it was my job to create a library of love, peace, and perspective that impacts me, the observer, and the recipient of the observer's new perspective. This book is only a tool into your journey of higher loving. This book encompass a small portion of what the last two tackled, but it webs everything together to leave your brain stimulated and your mind sparked with its main goal—to transform your life.

In this dream, I suffered like a man lost in sea, with no direction or water. Before I wrote *The Dear Queen Journey: A Path to Self-Love*, I was so lost and confused when it came this concept of self-love. Now, I look back, and I laugh and smile at the human and writer I was. I healed myself through the written word, and somehow it sparked this healing process in thousands of other people. I had no idea the words would balloon to become the healing project that it became, in the way that it has.

Why do I bring up this contrast? Because this book is not written from any source or pain. In fact, I am healed, happy, and motivated. I have overcome everything that was out to destroy me, and I live within a constant state of inner peace, love, abundance, and joy. I live every day with an unshakable belief in myself, my love life, and my future endeavors. My consciousness has risen to a place that can never be broken or shaken. I truly live with a constant inner peace and happiness. I am not closed minded to new ideas or experiences; I feel as if the love lane that I am living in is the most efficient one possible.

I am sharing this journey journal in the hopes that you, the reader, will always remain objective. I have asked and will always ask that you view this information as an objective perspective. No, I am not really the guru or expert. I am the person who is guiding you and exploring these topics with you so you can become the expert and guru of your *Dear Love Life*. You are the expert; you are the power. You are the one—the love of your life or the anchor of your stress. This book stands here as a guide to discover something deeper within you—true power, divine connectedness, and unwavering doubt. The text offers tools, skills, and assets that make you valuable to yourself and others.

Maybe you have an outcome or goal. I ask that you abolish it and allow the writings here to permeate deep within your core, as free of human expectation as possible. It's possible that your bias is the reason you're reading this book. It's possible and actually probable that you don't know anything at all, and that should scare you. True knowledge is having enough humility to admit that you don't know anything. Even when you do know, there is never enough knowing, because procedures, moods, and structures change. I admit to myself, daily and often, that I don't know anything. Knowing creates closed mindedness, and I don't teach that.

That is the realization I had to come to years and years ago; it transformed me, and it is the only reason I evolved as a human. It's because I admitted to myself that I didn't know anything at all and that I needed new knowledge and experience.

My spiritual journey of self-discovery and enlightenment started in the spring of 2009. It was then that I rejected everything I knew, especially around the topic of human relationships, motivation, and love. I sat there in a self-induced depression, and I was wondering why my expensive psychologist couldn't help me escape from these rabbit holes of hate and anger I was living in. This epitaph of reckless abandon, sexual promiscuity, and unconscious awareness continued for three years as I transferred my demons back and forth between the dark shadows of others.

In early 2012 I spent every single day living in the worst hell imaginable. I wasn't living inside of my purpose, my health was average at best, and my relationship situation was shaky. I was dating a girl who didn't give me life. In fact, she was toxic and added to the trauma. I had just lost my grandmother, my physical fitness suffered, and I was living check to check. At that time, all I knew was something had to change because the suicidal thoughts I had were happening more frequently. I never tried, but I had the thoughts, and that scared me. I knew that wasn't an option, and this was when I entered the self-help business. I was a writer my entire life, but it was then that I decided to write a book to help myself get out of the hole. I wrote two journals: *The Aggression* was a notebook full of anger and pain, and *The Forgiven* was a collection of letters I wrote to each person who caused me pain. I forgave them for the pain caused because I didn't want to suffer with the anger.

It may benefit you to do the same thing. I never published, nor will I publish, these journals because they are the tools that saved my life, and nobody but me needs to see them. I wanted to do something for the public that was similar, and in 2013 I started writing the *Dear Queen Journey* book. That book has helped thousands of people heal and grow; it was the first project that really got my name out. I share this because I feel it's imperative that you, the observer, understand where the narrator's writings and perspective are coming from. When we struggle, suffer, or are going through any type of pain, we cannot easily see the shift that may push us out of it. I'm letting you know I recovered and escaped that hell, and if you are there, you will too. I believe all humans deserve to be happy, to be successful, and to live in a lane of love abundance. Some do not believe they deserve that, but to me it is a right as a human being, regardless of age, gender, racial identity, or any other classification.

Lastly, and most importantly, I am not a nice writer. I am not here to appease anyone. Let's be honest—we've been blind and have accepted enough lies, half-truths, and fables that keep us away from activating the *Dear Love Life* lane that we truly want. I only want to be respected as the writer who is soulfully honest, introspectively thorough, and vividly transparent. If you're looking for someone to be nice and appease you, go online and find one of these beta-male writers who only posts quotes that tickle the fantasies of women across the world and who have abandoned reason and logic all in the name of gaining a female audience. Which truly says a lot about that content creator's ego, lack of understanding of a gift, and abuse of this power that we writers have. I am Sylvester McNutt III, a writer of raw truth, vulnerability, and openness. The text will challenge, question, and call out minute fragments of behavior, and that experience may be uncomfortable. There exists a great deal of peace, consistent happiness, and internal understanding that lives on the other side of that comfort zone.

As a reader you will not benefit from this book if you are easily offended—if that's the case, please suspend your ego before reading *Dear Love Life*.

In psychology and cognitive sciences there's something we refer to as "confirmation bias." It's a tendency to search for or to interpret information in a way that confirms one's preconceptions, leading to statistical errors. This is one of the most deadly tactics that we do, especially when it comes to our relationships and friendships. Any error or misstep in the observation or calculation of human behavior can lead to inefficient results.

Here's a real-life example of confirmation bias: Smoking cigarettes is not efficient for optimal health, and in fact it can lead directly to cancer, lung problems, and an unhealthy human body. However, people who smoke will typically light up with other people who smoke, for one main reason—they share the bond and confirm each other's biases toward the action. Doing so makes the users feel less guilty as they destroy themselves, regardless of what the activity is. The same thing goes for men who hang out with other men who cheat and degrade women. They attract the company of other males who feel like that behavior is acceptable because it helps them feel better about their choices. There's too much pressure involved for a man who wants to play those games while having a bunch of male friends who are married. They wouldn't allow him to live in their spaces comfortably.

Another example is petty, childish, and juvenile women who attract followings online with their hurtful, ego-serving, and destructive messages on love and relationships—the type of woman who says that "there are no good men." Of course she's going to attract other women who say that, because their biases confirm each other, thus perpetuating the victimization that they're practicing.

And think about a racist person who hangs around with racist people. These people group together because of their confirmed biases of hatred toward another race. It's easy to be racist when you have a tribe of irrational thinkers.

Becoming aware of this alone can change your entire perspective on everything. Confirmation bias is a natural and normal grouping that we do, but now you're aware. You can't unlearn something once you learn it. Confirmation biases can prevent people from creating and finding the love that they claim they want. Once the user accepts and introspects this concept of confirmation bias, then the user allows himself or herself to fully examine his or her own friendships, relationships, and most importantly, self.

Think about the Internet. Earlier, I referenced people who only post to appease their audiences. I beg of you to look at whom you follow online on your social networks. The accounts you follow have a direct correlation with how you live your life, on a very subconscious level. If you enjoy hearing, reading, or thinking about love and relationships, I encourage you to examine the pages you follow.

Please understand that as a writer, I've introspected and observed myself and peers. There are some writers who do not want to give you truth and perspective. Some exist to only appease one subgroup—which is sometimes women who blame men for all relationship missteps and who tell other women what they deserve. Please, just go examine the pages you follow. They could be creating unrealistic expectations for you and your *Dear Love Life*. As writers, content creators, and speakers, we have a great responsibility to make ourselves extremely aware of the words we tangle together. If you have body-image insecurities, I beg of you to unfollow these supermodels and perfect-body profiles that perpetuate and force you to think that you have to obtain this photoshopped body.

I urge you to unfollow and delete accounts that force you to keep up with the Joneses and push a lifestyle that corrupts your brain—causing you to think that spending an excessive amount of money is necessary for love, likes, or purpose. I implore you to delete and unfollow the writers, speakers, and self-proclaimed gurus who only blame one subgroup. The people who appease one and tease another. My friends, that is manipulation, and that is not really helping anyone. If so-called teachers, gurus, or writers can only appease you, my question to you (and them) is, how did they help you? It's possible that I myself may not make the cut; I'm prepared for that too.

This text is a part of a paradigm shift in your consciousness, with a focus on transforming your dating skills, conscious perspective of behavior, and levels of introspection with regard to relationships. It's imperative that we become conscious of the media we subject ourselves to. Every single song, episode, and rhythm contains a vibrational energy that tangles with our energy field. It's incumbent that we continue to feed our energy fields with media that uplifts, inspires, and motivates us to become more efficient or to accept and understand ourselves as we are.

Chapter 1

Love,

Awareness,

and

Consciousness

The New Mind-Set on Efficiency

The subtitle of this book contains a very important word: *efficient*. But does anyone know what this actually means? I am an observer of human behavior, and I listen to many humans explain their views on the world, and I've noticed that there is a big gap in understanding, awareness, and clarity.

Marketing gurus and experts use these types of phrases, and they make me shake my head every single time: "Be a good woman" or "Be a great guy." These phrases don't actually help the solution. They're just stating a perspective of the alleged obvious. Here's a hypothetical situation. Let's just say that you and I live together, and the rent is due on the first. Tell me which statement sounds more efficient to you:

> a. Rent is due on the first of the month. I do not have my half of the rent like we agreed upon.
> b. Rent is due on the first of the month. I do not have my half of the rent like we agreed upon. I'm seeking

unemployment. I called my brother who owes me money and has been doing better. The reason I do not have my half is because my daughter was sick and I had to pay for her medicine.

In this situation the problem is exactly the same. Most marketing gurus, and even us in our relationships, refer to the top as our form of communication, when in fact, the second is much more efficient and realistic.

Back to the introspection of the guru and marketing talk. The one that I really hate the most is this: "A real man does this or that." Without explain it further than that I become bothered. I despise it because it's a dumbing down of text, all in an effort to appease. We truly cannot grow and solve our dating problems with appeasement. We have to be honest and realistic with each other. The content creators have to be aware of this, and if they're not, then you are now.

Honestly, please help me understand: What is a real man? Logically, what does it mean? I have a physical body that can be touched, so does that make me real? If I get out of my desk in college and give my professor a hug, wouldn't that make her a real woman? The "real man" and "real woman" concepts are really clouding the ability to decipher healthy, safe, and efficient behaviors in a relationship. In fact, I surveyed 375 people to describe what they thought a real man or real woman was, and guess how many of the answers were identical? None. If there was such a consensus of what it means to be real, authentic, and genuine, isn't it a plausible assumption to make that we would all just be that, if we knew? What I'm alluding to is that an efficient, sustainable, and worthwhile partner will exhibit certain behaviors. For example, an efficient behavior is considering your partner's feelings before you act; communicating about problems before they become major or simply thanking your partner for his or her effort. One of the most important elements of a relationship or dating is to remain grateful for what you have, not to compare your lover or love life to the next person.

Please understand, introspect, and then accept this via your own observations too. If I told you what a real woman is right now, wouldn't it be subjective? Wouldn't it be based on my biases? Well, Sylvester likes women who are calm and have a sense of humor, so does that mean that a real woman has to have a sense of humor in order for me to deem her worthy? It's this type of illusory wording that has caused so much confusion and ruined our ability to date in the now, be in the now, and see things clearly as they are now. A woman who wasn't as funny as the next would still then be a "real woman," even though, based on my value system, she's not. This can't be summed up by making statements like "perception is reality," no. Again, another illusory phrase that doesn't deduce the truth.

There's no such thing as being a real woman or real man. There isn't one "good" or "bad" way to speak to someone, to behave, or to perceive things. Friends, I want you to explore this with me. Can you see where I am coming from here? I used the word *efficient* instead of *good*, *great*, or *amazing* because those words are just marketing terms and do not help our ability to be efficient. I don't suffer, and I don't want my readers to ever suffer in life, so my aim as a writer is to use language that resonates so there is no suffering. This book has a home in your heart and millions of others because we explore these truths together. It's not just some guru or expert on the other end telling you to live in a way that is unrealistic to you.

I want to be efficient as writer, and whatever you take from this book needs to be an implant of efficiency. Yes, you do deserve that. If you're not familiar with the true definition of efficiency, wrap your head around this: efficiency is a termed used to grade or observe a system that correlates the relationship between maximum productivity versus minimum or wasted effort.

What does this mean? I'm sure you've heard the term fuel-efficient cars, right? If you're into sports, you've heard about quarterback efficiency ratings or free-throw shooting percentages. Friends, every system has a measurable and observable level of efficiency. This is an axiom. If you build a company or if you go to your job, you participate in EBITA— earnings before interest, taxes, and amortization. This is a measurement that all companies and businesses use to measure profitability and efficiency. At no point ever are we exempt from efficiency or the idea of it.

Dating is a skill, being in a relationship is a skill, sex is a skill, breaking up is a skill, and communicating is a skill, and if you do not get coached, pay attention to the losses, or grow within your skill set, you will lose over and over.

Dear Love Life is a love-life backbone for any man, woman, or child. All users will benefit from implanting the mind-set that life and relationships are about efficiency. Once the user accepts that there is no such thing as a real man or real woman, and once the user starts to reject the rhetoric of unrealistic gurus and marketing experts, then and only then can this powerful mind-set permeate your soul and transform your life. I want your life to be transformed.

It's not about trying to be right, trying to prove points, or trying to get the last word in. To be successful in dating, you have to measure efficiency. Always start with yourself—always. This is why I have used the words

introspection and *consciousness* at least thirty times so far. Don't start measuring everyone else and what they're doing. You'll only create suffering. You're the one. You're the guru. You're the power, the source. Measure, observe, and watch yourself first and forever. If you practice remaining objective and honest, you can reduce most, if not all, of any problems that may occur in dating.

Become Aware of Suffering and Grow from It

The ego says, "I shouldn't have to suffer." And that thought makes you suffer so much more. It is a distortion of the truth, which is always paradoxical. The truth is that you need to say yes to suffering before you can transcend it.
—Eckhart Tolle

Suffering is the state of undergoing pain, distress, or hardship. Suffering is one of the underlying themes of the book. We often judge our environments and realities as good or bad and right from wrong. Unfortunately, there isn't a universal law of wrong versus right. If there was, we would all know it, live by it, and would be happy. The underlying theme to this book revolves around the concept that in dating, we must raise our vibrations and consciousness in order to alleviate temporary or permanent suffering. The point of looking for efficient and inefficient behaviors is so we can take the necessary steps to alleviate the suffering. Pain isn't fun. Suffering can last forever if we allow it. We don't need suffering. Suffering is stress. Science has proven that stress shuts down your immune system, which is your internal healing system.

The chain of understanding suffering is vital. When I mention suffering throughout the text, if you need a refresher, please come back to this page.

Suffering is a state. Think of it like a physical place that you visit, especially since it's connected to stress, and stress creates physiological changes in your body. Always remember this premise—it will transform you when you feel like you're suffering: If suffering is only a state, that means I have three options.

One, live there; two, visit there; three, watch it from the Internet. Suffering is a choice.

Personally, I live with a constant state of inner peace. I accept what is. I don't fight reality. I don't lie to myself about who or how I am. I don't tell myself I have flaws or weaknesses, as there's simply no point in doing that. It's more valuable and efficient to accept yourself fully as you are. You cannot identify a weakness if you do not accept it. That is suffering. A large part of our planet doesn't believe it's possible to accept and observe things as they are. This level of consciousness is what is needed in relationships, not control. Most seek control. Control is manipulation and suffering. Manipulation and suffering aren't love—they're stress and not worth anything.

What Is Overthinking?

Overthinking is the drug that plagues progress in efficient dating. In a practical matter, thinking is necessary. It's a subconscious event. If your friend says that you are overthinking, here is what the person is trying to tell you (you are person A, and your friend is person B):

B: I observe that you are going back and forth between outcomes and ideas. You are causing yourself a great deal of suffering and stress by doing this. Please stop overthinking.

A: How can you tell me not to overthink? Who sets the benchmark for thinking, and who can judge overthinking? Does this mean that there are people who underthink?

B: Yes, underthinking, logically, has to exist if we have a term to describe overthinking. Underthinking does not imply that one is less intelligent or that the overthinker is more intelligent. I notice that you're suffering, and I don't want you to suffer. Control: You're overthinking, especially around dating and relationships, because you think you can control all of the outcomes, and you cannot.

A: I like to have all of the facts, data, and observations so I can make the best decisions. I want to have clarity and understanding before I do anything.

B: That's valid, but it's unrealistic, in the realm of efficient relationships. It's also a great state of suffering. This idea of gathering data so you can be clear and understand is an illusory thought. You want all the data because you want a guarantee. You want a promise. That is suffering. You want to give yourself peace of mind by assuming that if you gather all of the facts, you'll be able to deduce all possibilities and all outcomes. That is obsessive thinking. That is suffering. There is no way, ever, you can predict all of human behavior. There are too many variables. I can commit to you, treat you well, and talk to you like royalty for ten years. That does not guarantee that it will happen on the eleventh year. Seeking a guarantee, promise, or fact is future suffering. It's present suffering. It's just a state of suffering, and you do not have to live there.

Your goal should be to gain an acceptance with what is. Focus on learning how to accept everything as it is now. If you focus on the now, you'll never go wrong. Each moment is the most important moment, not the moments in the future but the moments that exist right now. As an efficient lover, it is your duty to learn how to let go of the past and to not obsess about the future. You literally have to be present, in each moment with yourself and with your lover.

A: What about the future? What about plans? Sometimes I need to plan things. I am a person who likes to plan things out. Could this make me suffer more in relationships?

B: Planning is practical. Planning is necessary. Planning is a skill. Some personalities require planning because of how they were raised, or maybe their jobs force them to plan to be efficient. Nobody can reject that planning is needed. All logical conclusions have to accept planning.

Planning and overthinking are two concepts. They are different. Thinking is a part of planning because you need to think to plan, yes. That's fair and acceptable. You may plan a meeting: Roger brings the drinks, Melissa brings the pizza, and Jacob brings the paper plates. Planning creates expectation. Planning for others can be instant suffering because you create a space where another person needs to fit into your plan. This has the potential to be inefficient. You set a time for your party to start at 7:00 p.m. Jacob couldn't get to the store because of traffic, so he came to your place without the plates because he didn't want to be late. Now you're upset because your expectations weren't met. This is suffering. Both people will sit here, in this moment, and suffer. Jacob didn't want to disappoint you, but now he is upset with himself because he couldn't manage everything. You feel a certain way because your party is not going the way you want it to.

So how do they solve this situation? Is the planning, expectation, and obsessive thinking the root cause of the suffering? How do they resolve this? The only resolution is to accept what is. He couldn't get the plates because of certain circumstances. So do we remain upset and keep a hostile, confrontational relationship with him?

Do we continue, complain, and remain upset? An efficient person will let it go. In the grand scheme of happiness, it really does not matter. This is not worth arguing about. It is not worth telling him how unreliable he is. It is only about the present moment. Improvise. Eat off of paper towels, use your expensive china, or postpone the party and run to a neighbor's house. Eat in the kitchen. Overthinking and expectation will always lock you to suffering when things don't go the way you think. Your attitude should be to make the present moment your friend so you can adapt as these situations occur. This happens all the time in relationships. This is causation: expectation, expectations not met, suffering, arguing, and conflict.

I have a very important message for you: **you're going to die**. That shouldn't scare you. What should scare you is having a heartbeat, air in your lungs—but being figuratively dead on the inside. I no longer have the ability to watch the news, because it really makes me sad. Why does the news have to disappoint and upset us? People are dying every day. There's another scandal over here. This person is lying and stealing money from so and so, but XYZ major corporation isn't paying taxes and is firing hundreds of people.

Here in America 80 percent of people are living check to check, and 80 percent or more do not have an emergency fund with $4,000 or more. We are all broke and struggling to get by. Money is not the solution to happiness. Love is. I wish we could all be rich financially, but we cannot. Only some of us know how to create product, service, and purpose that can create true financial wealth. The rest of us have to struggle, and that's just the way this financial system is set up. If it was set up for us to all be rich, then there would be no rich, and our perspective of rich wouldn't even exist. I aspire to show you, through this text, that we can all be rich in love. There is no shortage. There is an abundance of love. Focus on feeling rich through love. Desire it; be it.

Please promise me that you will love and be there for your kids. Please tell me you will be loving and act like a bundle of love, because our world needs you, dammit. We need you to be a powerful source of light, love, and peace. The wars, fighting, and drama are not human life anymore, and it's time we start a revolution. A revolution based around love that has nothing to do with race, gender, or religion. We all deserve to be loved, and that is law. This is a human right. If you're going to support the revolution, contact me personally. Tell me that you're in!

How Do You Create an Efficient Relationship in the Technology Generation?

And then she sent a text message explaining how she felt, but he didn't understand her text message language. They both thought they were communicating with each other, but they were on different pages of different books. He called her, but she didn't answer because she was too busy at work.

But the girlfriend wasn't over her ex, so it didn't really matter, because they all were hiding, lying, and misleading the persons that they claimed they loved. This soap-opera, overdramatic scenario occurs all too often. Maybe you're guilty of this. I know I am guilty of participating in some of this madness too at one point or another in my life, and it's okay to admit it. However, it's not okay to bring this damaging, selfish behavior into relationship after relationship. Obviously, you and only you know your participation levels with madness. I'm willing to bet my next meal that the majority of us believe that cheating is wrong. I'm willing to bet that most of us believe that lying to people and manipulating others is wrong, yet so many of us lie, cheat, manipulate, and steal. This is your time to be real with yourself. There's no need to lie right now, because it's just you, me, and your consciousness. Of course, even though we may see something as *wrong*, that doesn't stop us, because some of the actions and behaviors feel so right to us.

Do you have a headache yet?

Because I do. I am so tired of the nonsense that we have allowed and participated in. My purpose for writing *Dear Love Life* is to shed some realistic perspective on dating in this generation. I feel as if we need to introspectively attack our dating expectations, behaviors, and perceptions. See, this generation is dealing with new tools that we truly do not understand. Social media, text messaging, and the amount of work that we participate in has created a void in love, and we have subjected ourselves to an unhealthy lane of solitude and entitlement that we cannot truly handle efficiently. As a result, we are jumping into rounds of survivor-series sex, the bottom of alcohol bottles, and bridges built on excuses and shadows of deceit. It's possible that you don't know what survivor-series sex is. In the 1990s, the World Wrestling Federation had a pay-per-view wrestling event, called *The Survivor Series*. I remember watching competitors destroy each other in the messiest, loudest, and most intense matches possible, just to win a prize. Ever since I was a kid, I've referred to sex as survivor-series sex. Think about how intense and aggressive we would be if every sexual encounter occurred because a championship title was at stake. This is the type of sex we jump into nowadays. In preparation to create this book, I interviewed hundreds of singles, nonmarried couples, married couples, and people who can logically explain their perspectives on dating in this generation. I interviewed single women and men from my tours as well as the committed lovers, and I even talked to people who are on the other side of love, heartbreak, and jadedness.

I will ask you, like I have asked every reader in every book, to read my material with an objective viewpoint. Being objective, literally, means that you're willing to take in the information without judging it based on your current biases. Keep an open mind, and view this material as a fly on your living room wall would watch you and your family interact. My goal as a writer is to get you to expand your consciousness; I want you to raise your vibrations and become the highest version of you, now and forever. So please, read everything objectively. Do not read this book saying, "I agree" or "I disagree"—nothing in these pages is seeking agreement or approval.

Actually, I challenge you with all of your endeavors not to seek agreement ever but to seek an understanding of all outcomes and perspectives. Agreement and appeasement is limiting; understanding is transformative.

Again, you must use objectivity here. The other challenge I have for you is to suspend the logical or, in some cases, illogical thought process that you currently have behind the judgment of "right" versus "wrong." Looking at things as right or wrong, again, is subjective because it is based on what you've learned or your personal biases. In order to observe anything objectively, you cannot look at things with a moral compass.

This form of human intelligence— thinking objectively—is one of the highest and can oftentimes be the most challenging because we are not taught to live or think in this way. For the duration of this writing, do it. The practice will leak over into your life, where situations allow, and you'll earn yourself relationships that contain much more peace.

As humans this is very challenging because we are accustomed to judging things because of survival. When it comes to survival, we naturally have to decide if a certain situation or stimulus is safe for us.

Chapter 2

Single, Dating, and Being Committed— Dating Types and Styles Defined

Dating Situations

In the realm of being efficient, it is necessary that we understand our situations and others' situations as we lend our hearts out to other people. I'm willing to bet that 60 percent of dating situations have problems because of one main reason: people do not understand what phases they are in. My friends, just like a newborn who turns into a toddler, who turns into a small child, who turns into an adolescent, who turns into a young adult, the dating cycle has phases. Here's the tricky part. Most of us don't know because we have unrealistic expectations, we lack the ability to clearly communicate, or we do not clearly observe and accept where we are. This text will help you remedy all of that. Key: this cycle is not a linear cycle. There are no rules that say one thing must happen in order for the next. For the sake of being rational and objective, please don't allow your mind to ponder on the one-off anomalies. There may be exceptions to the common. In a realistic world, most people do not fall in love at first sight and marry within the first month. Has that happened before? Of course it has, but is that the common behavior? No, so don't allow your mind to wander there.

Let's dive in. I highly suggest you take your own notes throughout this section. If I were taking notes, I would actually write down my dating situation now and past, with the people I was involved with. The reason I would do this is so I can compare and contrast so I can find my own truth throughout the text.

The new term "situationship" has been going around, but the behaviors of it are nothing new. A situationship is a situation where the two people who are sharing time and sexual benefits and resources are unsure and unclear of the arrangement and direction of the arrangement. This term is not good or bad, but it can lack efficiency because of the fact that in its core, a situationship lives in a gray area. In an effort to clear up the gray area, please understand that gray area is actually necessary and common in certain situations. Just because there is gray area doesn't mean anything is good or bad. You don't wake up single one day and then have a marriage and kids the following day. It takes time. Dating phases have to evolve naturally and not with force. The most important thing we can do here in this text, from a viewpoint of efficiency, is raise our vibrations around the layers of love participation. It's imperative that we truly understand our situations and others' situations so we don't get hurt and so we do not hurt other people. Let's introspect this more. There are only three levels that need to be explored: single, dating, or committed. You can only be in one of those phases. Let's look at them deeper.

Single

People who are single have no commitment, obligation, or involvement with anyone—they are not sexually active, and they are not emotionally invested in anyone. A truly single person is going to be the easiest person to start something new with. In our generation, we use the word *single* to imply that we are not in a committed relationship, and that is where the problem lies. **Single means no involvement.** If I go to the store and buy a chocolate bar and there's two pieces in there, that is a pair. They are together. There is no argument to this. If I buy a chocolate bar and it's one individual piece, then that piece is singular. Do we accept this?

When someone is single, there's no extra baggage or people who can play a part in the collateral damage of this person's life, because they're clearly uninvolved and unattached. This person can be fresh out of a relationship. She (or he) can be focusing on herself or can just be a person who doesn't jump from relationship to relationship because she is waiting for a particular person of interest to enter her life. If you meet someone who is truly single, pay attention and invest. This is the most rare person to find now, but the most valuable as far as starting something new goes. You'll have a highly effective life if you start a *Dear Love Life* entanglement with such an individual. I highly encourage you to approach him or her with open communication so you can develop trust and transparency. If you are single and you're emotionally available, you need to focus on being happy. The happier you are, the richer love you'll create and attract. You are the source.

Dating

This is the term that is used so loosely and the term that creates a lot of misunderstanding. The lack of understanding about what this term truly means is the reason why so many people are suffering with their dating situations and why they cannot escape. I hope I can bring some clarity to this. I don't want you to suffer anymore.

First and foremost, if you have any involvement with any person, you are dating. Dating is a verb. It is something that you're doing. Dating can also be a noun. It can be the place in which you see yourself—yes, the state of dating. If you are meeting up with Susan every Friday night and you guys are having sex, you're dating. You are not single. You are dating. If you have a guy who you are on and off with, meaning you are emotionally connected to him, and you guys try to be in a relationship and fail and try again and again, that is dating. You are trying to see each other. If you are on a dating site and you're messaging people in hopes of gaining dates, then you are in the act of dating. Dating does not mean that you are entitled to control or demand anything from anyone, and no one is entitled to demand and control anything from you. Dating means that both people are choosing to share space and energy with each other. Involvement means sexual meetings, emotional transfers, intimate conversations, and consistently speaking to someone while exploring the possibility of potentially reaching a commitment and relationship.

Dating often does not have a tittle. The lack of a clear title creates the gray area. Some people like to use phrases like "friends with benefits," "fuck buddies," et cetera. It's imperative that we understand that the title can and will always lead to confusion because this itself is a gray area. Logically, if you define a gray area with a title, it's still a gray area. The title is not what removes it from the gray area. It's the clear-cut communication from both parties that remove it from a gray area. Stop giving labels and titles to confusion. They will only confuse you more. This phase is dating.

Clear the confusion. You're single, dating, or committed. There are only three phases. Those are the only three phases; there is no gray area or confusion when you tell someone that you are in one of those lanes. Anything else is a subphase and will cause confusion. Dating means involvement without commitment. Got it?

Committed

To be committed is a state of consistently clearing up any confusion. There's no confusion when we are both willing to work, to grow, and to figure out our *Dear Love Life* together. There are different levels to a commitment. Legally, we can agree to a marriage. We can just be together and be boyfriend and girlfriend, but for the context of my writings, the title really doesn't matter too much. Individuals' personal beliefs, cultures, and religions will have a lot to do with how they perceive the different levels of commitment. I aim to make it much simpler than that: two people who have both acknowledged the commitment to each other have eliminated years of stress, problems, and confusion. I truly believe that over 50 percent of the relationship problems we have in this generation come when we are not in committed relationships. However, we are still exchanging time, emotions, and rounds of survivor-series sex. When there's no commitment there's so much room for the gray area, and people tip toe around this, until they force another person out of their life by violating the other person. I command you to believe in commitment. If you're scared of commitment, good. You're supposed to be. You're right. Relationships are scary, and you could be picking the wrong person. You don't know. However, you're going to use your discernment, you're going to trust your intuition, and you're going to take the risk because that's what life is about. No, you can't force anyone into a relationship, and you shouldn't aspire to. But you can have a mind-set of commitment and aspire to eventually create that. It feels amazing to know that someone has your back out here in this crazy, corrupted, and evil world. Love trumps all of that negativity.

What Is Dating?

In the very beginning, it should be about breaking the ice and finding out about each other's value systems. In the beginning, it also should be about being present in each date and interaction so the interactions can be genuine. Dating is a process of becoming friends. The dating process is sparked by interest, attraction, or desire— sexual, spiritual, or emotional connections based off of potential will be a motivating factor. Dating

is the natural process that each person takes to get to know, grade, and evaluate potential suitors to mate with.
—Sylvester McNutt III, *Dear Love Life*

Friends with Benefits Introspection (Dating Phase)—Some people connect so they can take care of sexual needs, and that is most often called "friends with benefits." Again, this is not a good or bad phase. We cannot judge what other people decide to do with their bodies. Who put us in the position of law, of moral judgment? It does not matter what moral basis we place our sexual behavior and commitment on, because that only applies for an individual, because this phase will exist no matter what. People are allowed to make whatever decisions they want with their bodies. Having sex outside of marriage doesn't make you a bad or hard person to date. If you wait until marriage, it doesn't mean you'll be a great husband or wife. We have to accept that people are allowed to do what they want. Judgment should not be passed here.

Some people do not have the skills, desires, or passion to get into committed relationships. However, all of us have human needs. If you start a friends-with-benefits situation at some point, it's highly possible that someone will develop feelings deeper than "just" a sexual interaction. Some people can look at sex as "just" sex, and some look at it as an entanglement of soul, a conglomerate of spiritual energy and an emotional connection that may never be broken. Each perspective is the truth to the holder of the perspective. Don't try to change anyone; understand your lover.

In fact, sexual interactions create emotional attachments. From my experience with some women, they feel like "after sex" the "relationship" has changed to "another level." This thought, which is understandable and realistic, will crush a lot of women if they do not understand this: men typically do not feel this way. Sex for a man does not mean the relationship is on a different level. It does not mean that he will care about you more. This text is not implying that all women will develop an emotional connection to the man after sex and that the man will not.

Scientists at Rutgers University have determined that during sex, thirty different parts of the brain can be activated in the female brain. While a woman is sexually aroused, her nervous system starts to shut down. This is why a woman can endure so much pain during sexual intercourse. That's why women associate the pain with pleasure. In fact, if you are a young man who has never had sex with a woman, be ready for her to basically ask for violent acts during sex. Nobody warned me that some women like to be choked, to be hit, or to be overpowered during sex. I was shocked and alarmed in my late teens when my girlfriends and such would ask for violence. I was always taught not to hit women, so for me, this brought a great deal of confusion. Now, in retrospect, and after education, I've learned that they associate said pain, from a trusting source, as pleasure. A key hormone released during sex is oxytocin, also known as the "cuddle hormone." This lowers our defenses and makes us trust people more, says Dr. Arun Ghosh, a GP specializing in sexual health at the Spire Liverpool Hospital. Women produce this hormone at a much higher rate, which is why they have a tendency to "fall in love" after sex, whereas men don't. Oxytocin does not tell us if this person is our soul mate, just a one night fling, or just an eight-month episode of heartache. The chemical only creates a deeper bond in women because they produce much more of it during sex. This is why choosing a sexual partner is vital to efficient dating. Sex for a woman will create a bond, and that's just the science of it.

Men aren't dogs. Men aren't full of shit. Men are biologically wired in a different way, and that energy has to be respected. If you didn't know, now you will know. Let me present you the facts that will help understanding. When men have orgasms, they release dopamine at a much higher rate than a woman does. Dopamine is a chemical that produces a feeling of pleasure and excitement. Dopamine, for men, does not produce anything that causes attachment other than addiction. This is why men become addicted to sex—dopamine alone has that power. Dopamine is what you experience when you get your direct-deposit notification on your e-mail or smartphone, when you get lots and lots of notifications on social media, or when people compliment your looks. That blushing or smiling feeling that occurs is a product of dopamine. Dopamine is excitement, not attachment. Stop calling men dogs because they have sex and because that is the end of their desire with women. Stop telling women that they are too clingy after sex. Now we know the difference, and this is the entire point of the book.

It's to understand that there is always another perception than the one that we currently have. I can't call my girl crazy and clingy after sex while knowing this information, because I know, because of biology, that she releases chemicals that make her that way. You cannot unlearn what you just learned. It will never leave you. A woman cannot get mad at me when I have sex with her and then genuinely just don't care what she does for the next week. I released chemicals of excitement and fun. We have to start to understand and accept each other's biology is different. It's imperative that we do this so we can stop jumping into these negative situations that ruin our happiness. This information is vital, and I encourage you to share this with your friends, your lovers, and your children. Do not wait for school to teach your kids these facts. Odds are, they'll have sex before you ever know. Here's an interesting fact from Dr. Ghosh:

> If you're struggling to nod off, it's better to have sex than to take a sleeping pill. "In fact, it's more beneficial to have sex in the evening rather than the morning because the body wants to be relaxed afterwards, not get up and go to work."

By having sex at the end of the day, you'll reap more of the stress-relieving benefits. For a man, a powerful orgasm is the equivalent of having on average a two- to three-milligram shot of diazepam (or Valium). That's why so many men nod off afterward—there really is a biological reason for this. A lot of sexual-health research focuses on what's happening physically. But experts say that for many people —especially women—the mind plays a key role in achieving orgasm. While male brains tend to focus on the physical stimulation involved in sexual contact, the key to female arousal seems to be deep relaxation and a lack of anxiety. The scans show that, during sex, the parts of the female brain responsible for processing fear, anxiety, and emotion start to relax more and more, reaching a peak at orgasm, when the female brain's anxiety and emotion are effectively closed down.

Once these feelings are realized, the user of this experience may not feel comfortable bringing up her new feelings. We think of all of the possibilities, and they scares us: Will they stay? Will they go? Do they feel the same way? Especially if the agreement was that it was purely sexually based adventure. This is why it's imperative to introspect your life daily; it's imperative that you make efficiency your duty. It's domineering that you employ logic, restraint, and understanding before you jump into these survivor-series-type rounds of sex. If you enter a friends-with-benefits situation, the worst thing you can say at any point is, "I'm not looking for something serious." Do not ever say this line, ever, to anyone, ever, under any circumstances. I guarantee you that this line will create conflict.

You indeed may not be looking for a serious relationship, but the second you say this, you're telling the other person that you've closed your mind to the idea of something more. This may be the truth, but after some survivor-series sex and time invested, that may change. That statement can and most likely will come back to bite you later in the form of conflict. If you start off as friends with benefits and then feelings develop, what happens when you close off the possibilities of more, and then feelings develop? The second that you express these feelings, you're committing cognitive dissonance, and this might jar the other person's reality of the arrangement

It's possible and probable the other person will have feelings and will be open to more too. However, I urge you to never say, "I'm not looking for anything serious or a relationship." The most efficient thing you can say is, "I'm not going to press you or anyone for a relationship, but I am open to exploring that when the time comes." When you say this, you release the pressure of a relationship, and you leave the idea open. Be genuine, and bring that type of energy at the beginning. Friends with benefits can often lead to a committed relationship and to marriage, but communication and transparency are completely required to make the transition. I assume that if you're reading this book, you do desire a committed relationship. If you're in a friends-with-benefits situation—you two are just meeting for sex—it's imperative that you focus on developing a connection outside of the sex. Sex is good. But naturally create opportunities to bond outside of sex. Create more consistent conversations. Lastly, understand that some people have no desire to go from friends with benefits to being in a committed relationship. Once the two desires no longer match up, it's okay to walk away only after you've given your best effort. You're never going to trick someone into a relationship via sex. It won't happen. Sex is readily available and easily accessible. So yes, that individual will find another partner, and if you get cut off because you only want sex, don't stress, because you'll easily find that. The demand for "just sex" arrangements is high.

Situationship (The In-Between-Dating Phase)—This phase occurs after the friends-with-benefits phase has taken shape and form. Time has passed, and now we view this as the gray area, which isn't good or bad. It's just how most people choose to view it. This type of expectation comes from the media and what we have been told about relationships. In this stage, feelings have arisen, people are sexually active, but there is no relationship commitment, and the two participating parities haven't actually talked about obtaining commitments from each other. One or both have desires to actually commit or be with the other person, but it's safe to say that one or both people may say, "I don't know what we are." Do not look at this as a bad thing, because sometimes forcing the relationship title or conversation can push people away.

One side of this story is that people refuse to commit further, even though they're still willing to stay as long as they can receive the benefits of another person. To get more on that, refer to the section where I talked about value system, attributes, and ratings. It breaks this down in detail. The situationship phase can be one day or several years, and there's not a single second of it that is bad. It's just unclear. If two people are happy in a situation that doesn't have a title that society feels like is necessary, who cares? My personal ideas on relationships revolve around the fact that those outside of a relationship cannot impact it with their mind-sets. It's up to me and her to determine what we are, how we are, and who we're going to be. I believe it is Oprah who has been with her beau for several decades, and they do not have the marriage title. Yet they publicly have a happy and efficient relationship. They are committed to each other. What people truly need to understand is that we are conditioned to chase titles and conditioned to chase the next thing. True efficiency revolves around living in the moment and being mindful of your day to day.

If you wake up every single day and attack your daily goals and ideas, after a month you'll abolish whatever goals you may have wanted to achieve, but it takes the ability to be in the moment and to appreciate what you have now. If you're sitting in a brand-new sports car that can go from zero to one hundred in four seconds, I'm sure you would want to show that off, right? You would love to prove to everyone that you have the best sports car, but is it necessary? Isn't there value in sitting at the red light, appreciating the clouds and the sun, looking at the wind blow and looking over to the beautiful person that is in the car with you? Or is it more valuable to worry about the strangers who are sitting at the red light, watching you two, who do not understand or even care about you? What's more important? You or them? If you predict, obsessively think, and try to plan instead of taking the daily action, you'll find yourself trying again every single month. The same thing applies to relationships. They all take time to naturally develop and grow into what they are. Don't be in a hurry to go from zero to one hundred. Speed bumps, speeding tickets, and accidents may happen on this course of dating, but you'll live, and you'll drive again. Also, please understand that nobody else's relationship path has anything to do with yours. Some meet, get married in six months, and divorce a year later. Some meet as kids, marry others, get divorced, and find each other later in life. Some meet, travel the world together, never get married, and love each other until the end of time. Everyone has a different and important course. Some people have never had relationship conversations from the standpoint of "What are we?"

They just simply start referring to each other as each other's better half or partner. Actually, that is the tactic that I have always done my whole life. After spending time with and getting to know a woman I like, I just say, "Hey, you're my girlfriend." If she says no and disputes it, then we can talk about it, but 95 percent of the time it works. The one time it didn't work, she actually never talked to me again and moved to Colorado. We were dating for about four months, and everything was going well, until I told her that she was my girlfriend. She did not want commitment at all. Yes, she was at my house every single day. Yes, we were having sex, sharing resources, and I really liked her. However, in her head we were friends with benefits, and in my head I wanted to be in a relationship with her. This is what happens all the time to people. Just because you like and care for someone doesn't mean you both want the same thing, and that is okay. I'm happy that she left and moved, because it gave me the space to invite a woman into my life who actually wanted to be there.

Ultimately, there isn't one particular way that a happy relationship will go. It's relative to the individuals, so to expect more than what you have, if both people are happy, might be greedy and selfish. Greed and selfishness are potential components of relationship death. Introspectively, it was selfish of me to expect that she wanted to be in a committed relationship with me. We had only been dating for about four months. Is that selfishness wrong? Absolutely not. It's natural and felt like the right thing to do.

I urge you to be very careful pushing for the next phase in your relationship, because naturally, phases change as they're supposed to based on the growth of the two people. Your goal as a reader of this text is to examine yourself from a communicative and behavioral standpoint. To win in a relationship, one has to understand psychology, outcomes, and behavior. We are pretty much all in tune with how we feel, because we feel it whether we accept it or not. We still feel it, and that makes you in tune with yourself. What we do not understand is understanding itself—understanding of interpersonal relationships and human motivations. Society is what is telling you to force titles, and if you want the title, that's okay too. This text is not here to say that you shouldn't go after what you want, if a title and commitment are what you want.

If you want to be married or in a committed relationship and would like the title, let's talk about that next. You have to accept and understand that everyone is not your soul mate or the one for you. You have to understand that dating makes you a better partner *if and only if* you learn about yourself in the process. Most people lack the skills needed to be married, and dating is actually the process that helps you learn those skills. Don't knock dating, because it's necessary. Our generation has concocted this microwaved relationship idea that we can just manifest love out of nowhere, and that is so far from the truth. You can't just hit the timer for three minutes and expect love to be ready. That'll never happen. If you want your expectations to get met, you need to fully understand reality. If you have a flawed perception or biased view of behavior, you will always cause yourself a state of suffering in your love life. You will create unrealistic expectations that will ruin your daily happiness. You cannot expect anyone to think how you think, act how you would, or to respond to situations in a manner that you would. Your heart, logic, and perception of life will always deduce a different outcome than them. Be open-minded and easy to communicate with. Let go of expectations of others and only hold expectations of self. There can be no disappointment with this mindset.

The Seven Dating Styles

A great deal of conflict comes from casual dating and expectations and a lack of understanding what type of daters there are. I will argue that expectation is the root of all suffering. To expect means to protect and to try to manipulate a situation. There aren't any humans who can truly control another human without force or threat of life. To a degree, we have free will. Obviously environmental impositions and influences waver the true essence of free will, but we still make the choice regardless. Most humans date differently. There are people who date like you, but you may meet someone who dates differently, and it's imperative that you imply awareness and understanding.

The goal is never to change someone's dating style and preference. The goal is to understand your own views and theirs. Once there's a few conversations about this, it becomes so much easier to adjust and to adapt to each other. If you want your expectations to get met, you need to fully understand reality. If you honestly believe that everyone out there dates the exact same way you do, then you are sheltered and probably a little closed minded. You will suffer because of this. From the sample data I've gathered, couples I've helped, and people I've introspected with, I believe there are seven different types of daters.

It's imperative that you know exactly where you stand, because as life goes on, you'll change your dating style. Dating styles change because environments, maturity, and desires change. I highly doubt you would date the same way now that you did ten years ago. You grow; you learn; you prosper and elevate what you expect and what you bring to the table. Here's a list of the most common daters I see in this generation, each with a description and analysis on what makes their dating style unique.

Seven Dating Styles Explained

Solo Daters - They believe that the dating experience should highly resemble the relationship experience. They will be monogamous and date one person at a time. They can easily feel like loyalty is missing if they deal with any other style of dating.

Speed Daters - Fun—they don't take anyone too serious. They love going out and being social. They make out casually with someone and exchange numbers a lot. Typically, younger daters fresh out of college or even in college. They're not really looking for anything serious.

Building Daters - Some of the hardest people to date. They value work, school, or personal achievements more than they care about building relationships. These people will always be financially okay, successful, and praised, but they often suffer in relationships because they lack detail and focus. They're hard to pull away from their jobs, because they feel like work defines them.

Tornado Daters - Very simply put, they are married, in relationships, or in emotionally enticed situationships, and they're looking for an out. They don't care who they hurt. They just need to escape. They'll piggyback anyone who gives them a chance, because they don't want to be alone. Mixing your life with them will create an emotional tornado.

Playing-the-Field Daters - For this generation, these are the most common types of daters. They most likely believe in committed relationships, but they also believe in dating multiple people. Playing-the-field daters needs to date multiple people to compare and analyze how they think they're going to work out with potential partners. They truly do look at it as a process of elimination. From a numbers perspective, the playing-the-field daters are going to have higher chances at finding the right partners because they're testing a larger pool. This is their logic. You won't change it. Dating for them is fun; they enjoy it. They have to be convinced to begin a relationship via their own conclusions from their logical gatherings. It needs to logically make sense to them

Jaded Daters - These daters have the most negative mind-sets on dating. They're victims. They say things like this: "All men are dogs" and "Women aren't loyal out here anymore." They're fresh out of breakups, depression, or intense losses. They are not in healthy spaces. These people look for others to date so they don't actually have to face their problems. They think getting in relationships will satisfy them, when what they're doing is setting up new people for destruction.

Relationship-Minded Daters - These daters believe in commitment and monogamy. They openly express their desires to commit and to be committed to. They're often single because they don't like the dating process. They've forgotten that in order to get into a relationship, dating must occur. They don't want to waste time with

people if they're not going to marry them. Often for them, marriage is the biggest goal.
Sometimes they get so trapped into wanting a relationship that they push people away or cut people off at any sign of fear. They can be guilty of putting "too much" pressure on people.

Dating Archetypes Described: How They Work with Each Other

It's important that we introspect the different dating styles and understand how they work with each other. Below, I'll list an analysis of observations that I have made of my clients, people who have spoken at my shows, and the hundreds of e-mails I get per day. One of the biggest issues that I see now comes down to understanding dating styles.

It's safe to say that the generations before us dated in a very linear, well-understood way, but we don't truly know because we weren't there. Ultimately, the past really does not matter. The problem is that most of us do not understand our lanes or the others' lanes. I will introspect each lane to show you the benefits. With each description, I'll speak on compatibility issues that I've noticed. Remember, this is about dating styles. Once you're in a relationship, this isn't as important because the general idea that we're all going to agree to is that committed relationships equal commitment. In this text, the problem most people have is that they're not getting to the committed-relationship phase anymore. **There's a disconnect**. People are getting stuck just dating. People are breaking up with people who they're just dating, and that should never happen. This is a serious problem with our generation, so let's stop the madness and start by understanding the evolving lanes and changing moods, and let's bring these styles into our awareness so we can dominate our *Dear Love Life* experiences.

Dating is about psychology; the more you understand, the more efficient you will be. I challenge you to always come back and visit this section of the book when you're dating. This will help you understand exactly what you're getting yourself into. The common goal is to get to a relationship commitment with a person that you truly enjoy. Everyone has a different perspective. It's also worth noting that an open mind, in dating, is the only mind that will attract the true love life that we claim we want. For example, my dating style is called Playing the Field, and my woman is a Solo Dater. In our situation, once our feelings got involved, we introduced conflict into our dating experience. She wanted me to only date her, and I wasn't ready for that. I still wanted to date other people because I hadn't deduced that she was the one I was supposed to commit to. In some cases, people run when this happens because people's ideologies do not line up. Here is a full explanation of the different ideologies that I believe are most common and ways to manage, cope, and cooperate with the others. No matter what you think, people are dating in different styles than our parents' generation. Adapt or keep getting hurt. Those are your choices.

Dating is about psychology; the more you understand, the more efficient you will be. If you refuse to learn behavior, including your own, you will suffer. At this point, dating ineffectively is a choice. Learn, grow, and adapt or keep getting hurt.

Solo Daters

They believe that the dating phase should be very similar to the relationship phase. In fact, to them, those two phases are almost the same process, minus the commitment. They believe that monogamy is key and also like to practice this in the dating phase. They date one person at a time; they're sexually active with one person at a time. This dater only needs to judge his (or her) experience with this one person to decide if he wants to go into a relationship. Solo daters are often loyal and easy to be with. Their dating style allows you to feel their loyalty and love.

The have strong expectations of others, and often these expectations will cause them a great deal of stress and strife. They do not mesh well with other dating types that do not align the way they think dating should go. Their dating style is archaic and does not truly reflect the paradigm switch that this generation is leading. They will often try to force playing-the-field daters to not go through their dating process because they don't see the value in that dating process. They think playing-the-field daters are typically disloyal, dishonest, and selfish, which is not true.

Solo daters have the easiest time getting to know people because they don't invest their time in multiple places or people. From a mathematical-equation perspective, this person has the lowest possibility of finding the right match. Yes, these daters are picking quality partners, in their minds, but their dating fields are so low and they meet so few people that in most cases they suck at dating.

If you're a solo dater, your main goal should be to choose a quality partner. Check that —your main goal should be to be a quality partner because you're not going to create many opportunities for yourself. In my personal experience with solo daters, they have to understand that others may not see dating their way. I mentioned earlier that my woman is a solo dater. She wants to date one person at a time, and she does this based on her logic. In her logic, dating should be like a relationship. I am a playing-the-field dater. Her logic literally does not make any sense to me. Why would I want to treat you like we are in a relationship when we are not? What if I deduce that I actually don't like you in that way? Then we have to try to be just friends, and you'll feel like you were led on and used. That's not the case. As a solo dater, just be aware that other dating styles may offer you a great deal of conflict. This does not mean that the person you're dating doesn't want to be with you. He may just need a little bit more time. With respect, communication, and activities of trust, this process will be seamless.

Speed Daters

Fun. All they want is fun. Fun doesn't mean just sex. It means fun. It means that the definition of fun is not being in a committed relationship. Any person who says "I do not want to be in a relationship" immediately gets grouped into the speed-dater group. Why? Because this individual literally rules out the possibilities of commitment, deep-time investment, and consistency. A speed dater does not want to be changed. This person is more inclined to participate in the hook-up culture, often having situationships and noncommitment types of encounters. This dater genuinely does not want the pressure of a relationship. He or she doesn't have the energy or mental focus to invest in one right now.

If you try to date a speed dater, you must, and I mean you absolutely have to, respect the fact that she (or he) communicated to you that she wants fun. Trying to force her into a relationship when she wants just fun is stress and pressure and is not fun to her. She will distance herself from you. If you develop feelings and attachment to this person, it's fair to say that you may be able to convince her to like you in that way. But it's highly unlikely that she will. Speed daters want fun. Be their fun. If you represent anything other than fun, they may go elsewhere.

As a speed dater, it is your man goal is to always be as honest as possible about your behavior. If you're just trying to get sex and have no desire for a relationship, make that clear and apparent. The hardest speed dater is a person who allows people to fall for him (or her), knowing from day one that he had no intention for more. There's a working stream of communication between a speed dater and his partners. The most important goal for transparency should be that you communicate clear and effective messages. You can save a lot of hearts by making it clear that you just want fun.

You will set yourself up for failure if you expect a speed dater to settle down. Will he eventually settle down? Yes. Will he settle down with you? It's possible. But, if he has made it perfectly clear that he wants fun, including being friends with benefits, do not expect to change him. Do not think that you'll be able to convince him to switch his dating style just for you. This is simply madness. You will hurt yourself.

If you only want to have a sexual connection, don't be scared to say that. Don't lie to others to get their benefits. Tell them what you have in mind. Protect your integrity and their hearts by being honest. If you date for fun, respect the fact that fun for another can turn into genuine emotion and care.

Building Daters

These are some of the most lucrative and attractive daters that you'll ever see. They understand business and motivation and have the go-getter mentality. This person is extremely focused on leveling up her (or his) education, getting a career that rewards her, or pushing for some astronomical goal. This person is hell bent on achievement. She does not have the "I don't want a relationship" mind-set, but she doesn't really think about it, because she's building, and building is the most important priority right now.

I'm willing to bet that people who are building are also in another dating lane too. I'm willing to bet that they are either speed daters or they are the relationship types. Yes, you can, in some cases, have a blended dating style. Some are more concrete than others, but some people have slightly blended styles. A person who works forty hours per week, goes to grad school, goes out on the weekends, and works out at the gym during the week does not have time for a relationship (in his or her mind). These builders have made themselves so busy with life that there's not enough perceived time left to explore relationships. As a result, they're either looking for fun or relationships, but they don't want either one to disrupt their building phases. That is the key component to understanding this perspective. **They genuinely do not want their building phases disrupted**, and they will cut anyone off who doesn't complement the building phase.

These types of persons will always be successful, financially motivated, and secure in who they are. They take time to work on goals. In fact, daters with this mentality will have highly attractive abilities and traits. If they apply 70 percent of that energy toward building relationships, they'll be relationships that are worth a damn. These are a great daters when they put themselves out there, because they also won't allow their time to be wasted. Dating for them is a chore, so when they date, they're usually putting their best feet forward and making genuine efforts to see people.

If you try to date someone who is focused on building, it will also benefit you to figure out how you can help them build, and is it possible that you two can build together? A lot of power couples build deeper bonds by sharing and building businesses together. Maybe you two share a food blog, do personal-training boot camps together, or participate at a local church together. The medium doesn't matter—all that matters is that you build.

But beware, trying to be with someone

who is obsessed with his (or her) work can make you feel second place. You may never feel important or like you're as valuable as his work. It's truly up to the building-phase dater to be conscious of the concept of balance. If you're a building dater, you have to respect people when they're trying to share intimate space with you. At lunch and dinner, stay off your cell phone, and engage with them.

Nobody truly wants to walk on eggshells, and nobody prefers to feel like her work, hobby, or passion isn't valuable. Yes, dating and getting into a relationship take time, so you're going to have to sacrifice time if you want it. If you're halfway entertaining people because of a busy schedule, ask yourself a few questions: The material things—the status or purpose that you work toward—do they allow you to have work-life balance? If it does not, what true value are you getting out of it? Are you just a slave to status, to money, and to working hard, and if so, why? Do you not believe that relationships are rewarding?

As a building dater, I encourage you to pay attention any time someone genuine is actually trying to bring you back down to earth. It's truly rare that anyone will try to pull you out of your own way (99 percent of the building daters are in their own way). You're not bad at dating. You just don't think about it as much as the next. Yes, you think about it on those lonely nights, but you're stoic and somehow just keep pushing for your goals. Breathe...

At lunch and dinner, stay off your cell phone, and engage with them. Nothing on the phone is as valuable as the true connection of conversation. Attention and focus are essential keys to building a healthy relationship.

- Sylvester McNutt III

Tornado Dater

I don't recommend this person date anyone, but this is a large part of our broken generation, so let's bring some perspective to this dating style. If you're a tornado dater, you need to focus on self-love, self-awareness, and growth away from toxic or negative situations. I believe you should be investing in self-help books, a spiritual journey, or be going through some type of lifestyle transformative phase. You are growing from some type of trauma or loss.

Tornado daters are prone to codependency. They jump from person to person, throwing their bodies at people, just trying to get what they can. They lack true identities for themselves, and they don't know what they want. They'll go with the flow of whoever is providing the flow, even if that means they have to suffer a little bit. Or if they have manipulative tendencies, they'll create worlds around you that almost seem too good to be true. A tornado dater truly lacks self-love, self-awareness, and self-worth because he doesn't care if the person he's interested in already has a relationship.

As far as suffering, peace, and longevity, these are not concepts this person thinks about. She has a self-serving, if-I-want-them, I'll-get-them attitude, even if the other person is committed to someone else. In this generation, we use slang terms to describe this person: scumbag, slut, whore, ho, fuckboy, thot, side girl, or side guy. These terms will go away, and they will lose relevance. For the sake of understanding, they refer to a person who violates the common standards of dating or relationship perspectives. As this book gets passed down through generations, you can adjust the words to match.

A tornado dater does not mind breaking up a relationship, hiding the relationship, or building it while another is committed. The true essence of tornado dating means that a person doesn't mind creating stress to date. It doesn't make the individual a bad or unworthy person. It just means that he or she is willing to create stress.

I truly believe in my heart of hearts that most people would like to be in a committed relationship that is fun and rewarding.

With tornado daters, it feels like they just don't know how to efficiently go about it. It feels like they may lack the skills and the know-how to distinguish destructive behavior from nondestructive behavior.

A tornado dater can be all the way in another dating lane but then arrive here via emotional cheating, violent tendencies, or reckless abandon. **Any person who**

consistently and knowingly practices toxic behaviors is a tornado dater.

Why do you keep going back if you already know he (or she) will treat you like you're less than dirt? Why do you make excuses for a person who shows you hate every day, even though he claims to love you? Why do you keep cheating on your woman if you promise her that you're going to be loyal? Why do you keep checking your man's phone and stalking his social media account if you promised you wanted to build trust? These are just questions to pinpoint behaviors. These behaviors start the tornado process. Anything that is consistently toxic is a tornado. Any behavior that will start a tornado-like effect is toxic and what we need to avoid. We all, at some point, do something that is wrong or bad for our relationships. It becomes a catastrophe and tornado-like once we keep exhibiting any behavior that we know produces a negative outcome.

At any point in dating, either single or in a relationship, we can practice the ways of the tornado. The way you stop the tornado is self-awareness and introspection. Daters of every lane need to be honest with themselves, and they really have to see how their actions may impact their worlds. If they do not reflect and use awareness, then they're just walking pools of destruction, waiting to ruin every heart, job, and person they talk to.

Odds are, tornado daters have no clue they live this way.

We all, at some point, do something that is wrong or bad for our relationships. It becomes a catastrophe and tornado-like once we keep exhibiting any behavior that we know produces a negative outcome. To create a tornado inside of our lives, knowing the outcomes will be toxic, dangerous, needs to be stopped immediately.
- Sylvester McNutt III

Playing-the-Field Daters

They look at everything logically. Their
dating process is about logic, business, and
process of elimination. The process of
elimination is a scientific approach to solving a
problem. It is a method to identify an entity of
interest among several ones by excluding all
other entities. These daters are using a fact-
based, science-based, and experience-based
approach to dating. They need time, proof of
consistency, and value before they will think
about commitment. During the dating phase,
they don't get obsessively attached, because it's
not natural to be too emotional too fast. No,
they're not cold and heartless. They will feel
emotions and develop emotional bonds, but it
takes time.

It takes time because they want to date, or
will date, more than one person at a time in
order for them to go to the commitment phase of
dating. For them, they will not date in any other
way because they don't actually want to. A
playing-the-field dater can be man or woman,
can have the desire to be in a relationship, or can
be just a casual dater. This archetype doesn't
want just fun or just sex. These daters want

more. They desire relationships, but they go about it casually, without pressure or force. This is the most important thing to remember—a play-the-field dater truly desires to be in a relationship.

This dating style, in this dater's head, gives him or her the highest percentage at picking the right person. In fact, these daters have no problem allowing two people to develop feelings for them, and they'll see how it feels to be with one or the other. Dating is used to compare and analyze so they can pick the right person, which is the most important thing to them. They feel strongly about relationships and commitments, but it has to be a process of elimination. The one variable that matters, obviously, is the person's access to a dating pool. Playing-the-field daters can be solo daters too. They don't mind dating one person at a time if the opportunity presents itself. If this dater is in a situation with someone—noncommitted, a situationship—she (or he) has no issues dating a new person, because she doesn't feel as if the person she's with is commitment worthy. In some situations, she needs to see that nobody is better than the person she is dating. An honest, admirable play-the-field dater will be honest during this process. If you date someone who believes in playing the field, there's two things that you can do to protect your happiness: accept that this person dates in this way, and give your best to him or her.

These daters are grading logically and not based solely on how they feel. You convince them with logic—logic based on their value system of commitment. Don't try to force someone to be a solo dater just because you are one. On the other side, I have a very important paragraph to bring you.

Performance Compensation—I see this happen all of the time. It occurs when people do not align from their dating styles, and one person assumes that he (or she) needs to give all they have to earn extra credit. You'll see that emotions are involved, and one dater thinks that the only way to convince this person to actually commit is to go above and beyond what he or she would normally do. This is failure in a bottle. Never do this. Do not give what you do not have. It will haunt you and will create pressure on the person you are dating to reciprocate our energy. You truly have to be patient and allow them to go through their natural process. Do not compensate for another person's lack of interest or try to figure out what he or she wants. They have the choice to or not to communicate effectively. All you can do is be your best, communicate, and remain open-minded. Be your natural self and allow the divine order of the universe to play out. It will be okay, but force via performance compensation is emotional suicide for you. Don't do this.

"In dating, there are no promises or realistic guarantees. Never fall for a person's promises or talks of the future, in fact, you have no real reason to make such claims either. The only thing that matters is how you treat them and how they treat you, today. Always focus on building in the now and remaining present with each other. Present behavior can tell you a lot about how the future will turn out.

- *Sylvester McNutt III*

Jaded daters cannot breathe well inside of any dating lane. They have a terrible time dating people because they navigate their dating perspectives with a hurt, jaded, and pessimistic mind-set. They think about pain more than progress. They think about their victimization and their terrible outcomes. If you are a jaded dater, then the number one thing you do is attract negativity by talking about it and by believing in it. A jaded dater can be fresh off of a break up or can be a person who has never healed from a traumatic situation. I highly recommend that that all jaded daters remove themselves from the dating scene because you are not operating at a frequency that we like. You don't like it, and I don't either. You're attracting people who are operating at a low vibrational frequency, and it's because you live there too. It's time for us to remove ourselves from the jaded-dater category, and here's how:

Step one, start to practice physical fitness, daily, and keep it consistent. Step two, remove the mind-set that keeps you enslaved. You're no longer allowed to think that everyone is going to hurt you simply because one person hurt you. Step three, you're going to actively pursue positive mind-sets and situations that allow you to practice positivity. Your mind-set is the most important factor in dating. I've noticed that a lot of jaded daters are actually codependent because they seek people who can heal them. They search for happiness inside of other people, and that's not fair. You will hurt all parties involved if you date while still dealing with unresolved grief, strife, and depression. I do believe that love can heal and can change the course of those feelings. That love needs to occur internally first and always before it should be searched for.

If you're in pain, jaded, and fearful of dating, then your mission is to heal. The only way that you'll get the love you want is by paying attention to your own red flags and dealing with your problems before you take them to another person. Nobody deserves to inherent a duffel bag of problems. Heal so you can feel the greatest feeling: love. **The jaded daters fear introspection and reflection because they make toxic look so damn beautiful.** Growing and changing may make them ugly, and they don't want to deal with that problem.

If you're toxic I guarantee you will attract, will add, and will multiply the amount of toxic that exists inside of any relationship.

Being Committed Defined

(Commitment Phase) The quest for millions of lovers is to obtain commitments from the people they are dating. The commitment actually comes with several components that in this generation are often overlooked and not talked about. When I speak on commitment, here are the core values and behaviors that determine and keep efficient relationships alive and thriving:

HealthThe first commitment both people should agree upon is one to encourage and nourish each other. It's possible that you have buried one of your parents, and if your life is anything like mine, you buried your parents *too soon*. My father was only fifty years old when he passed, and I believe one of the major components of his demise was his lack of health. Health—when you mention that alone, people think you're talking about going to the gym, which is hard and takes a lot of effort. In fact, I'm not referring to going anywhere. I am only talking about where you are at.

For a relationship to be efficient, it is imperative that health be a major commitment. Both parties need to have a focus and desire to want to be happy as individuals and then as a unit. You cannot achieve happiness with another if you're tearing yourself apart every single day. Two happy people should start dating—then they can become one happy unit. There needs to be a commitment to fun and happiness, which is a part of emotional health. Oftentimes we slave away for our corporations and not for ourselves. I know everyone needs to pay bills and earn money; we can accept that. However, most of us work way too much. Most of us have paid time off from our jobs, and we're not using it. Most of us do not travel, explore, and grow once we get in relationships. We allow our spirits to die because we get comfortable and lazy.

I command you to force and train yourself to make the daily time necessary for your relationship to blossom. Both people need to recondition their brains and subtract this mind-set that obsessively working is the goal and is necessary. The mind-set should be that we both want to encourage each other to be happy and to enjoy happy moments with each other. That's the way to develop, continue, and allow emotional health to dominate you. In too many relationships, too many people are emotionally cheating, and to me this is relationship death. This occurs because people do not develop communication and respect parameters at the beginning of the dating stage. It is vital that you communicate openly, no matter what, from day one. Most people are guarded because they're not confident in who they are. I command you to be confident in who you are, because confidence leads to an increased level of attraction. An increased level of attraction means the person you're dating will want to communicate more because he or she will value you more. It's up to you to make sure that you communicate openly and honestly from day one. Once you do this, then and only then do you have a chance at fighting emotional cheating. It's plaguing the majority of relationships I see now, and most people will not admit to it, because they're justifying it via their own biases and insecurities. Another pillar of commitment is what I call "physical presence."

Have a Commitment Conversation

When you decide to enter a relationship, I want you and your partner to repeat this phrase over and over. It will help embed the depth of what it truly means to be in a partnership. Just say, "We are committed to the commitment." The idea is that as long as we work daily on our commitments, we can't lose. This culture and idea can take over the individual and the entire relationship entity. All of your commitments will change, but there is no reason to void a commitment simply because life has changed a little bit. I practice this in my own relationship and share this tactic with the people I have counseled over the last few years.

It's a self-hypnosis practice and will actually help you stay focused, mentally strong, and committed to the test of your relationship. When you are married, depending on the type of ceremony, you will have vows that are said. Whether married or not, I find it valuable, important, and mandatory that both partners revisit their commitment views, renew them, and speak to each other about commitment. Have a "commitment" conversation with yourself first and then your partner. If things are going well, it should only get better by restating and reviving your commitments. This self-hypnosis tactic increases the experience and makes each person want to live up to a higher standard. If things are not going well, bringing up new commitments can actually help because it can create a sense of purpose, can give direction and clarity to the design of the relationship.

Sometimes we fall a little bit shy of the lifestyle we want because we don't actually set targets or talk about what we want. This type of conversation gives couples the ability to realistically audit their relationships and, most importantly, their commitments to them. We know lots of people, who are in relationships, but they're not actually "in the relationship," and you know exactly what I mean. I do believe that being in a relationship is only effective once both people can communicate clear and effective messages to each other without judgment. The second part of this commitment conversation is the honesty.

It might be very possible that your desire to progress forward in the relationship may have vanished. It's possible that you may need to ask your partner about how well or poorly you're doing as a partner. It's possible that you'll have to tell your lover about his or her areas of opportunity. All in all, use a commitment conversation as a way to give your relationship and oil change. The dynamic of your relationship depends on how you want to strategically go about this. Some can just have a casual conversation full of laughter and joking. Others may want to take notes, to write things out, to have it be a more formal gathering. Some may reject the idea altogether because they want to be free of control, structure, and rigidness. Having a commitment conversation is necessary when you start the relationship. Many individuals commit to being boyfriends or girlfriends, but they never actually ask what their partners expect or believe to be the purpose for the commitments.

Most couples fail because they go from dating to being in a relationship, and they don't define the differences that will keep them together. If you don't want your lover talking to her (or his) ex every night at 11:00 p.m., this conversations should be had before you guys agree to be in a committed relationship.

If you've never mentioned that a particular behavior bothers you and then you commit to her, understand that in her head, you are okay with all of her behaviors . Pick your poison. Some things do not need to be mentioned and some do.

For example, my girlfriend doesn't like that I can get by with one plate, one cup, one knife, and no paper towels in the kitchen. This honestly is not a big deal to me, and it's not going to make her become uncommitted to me. However, she doesn't like when I don't clearly communicate with her. This is something that she has expressed is vital in her ability to be happy with a relationship. Because of the fact that she expressed it, I try to take it into consideration every single day. The next time we talk about our relationship and commitments, I will ask her if I'm communicating well enough for her. This will let me know exactly where I stand with her. She has a few things that she is working on for me too.

This is why I believe commitment conversations are 100 necessary for a relationship to thrive. Banks send statements once a month. You take showers daily because you accumulate dirt. Report cards come out every quarter. These are all progress reports and check-ins. Don't live your *Dear Love Life* on autopilot. Give yourself a report card and talk to your partner about the relationship. It matters.

Physical Presence

This is the pillar that other people can measure and that will cause you the most confusion because it appears to be tangible. *Physical presence* implies that the parties will communicative via face to face, phone call, text messaging, social media, e-mail, handwritten letters, or any other way that we can communicate in this generation. Do not misinterpret the text. It's not saying that daters have to communicate on all of these mediums. It's saying that they'll be more inclined to want to communicate on whatever mediums are perfect for their arrangement.

The second level of physical presence is commitment around sexuality and desirability.

I see so many people jump into relationships even as they forget that one of the major components is attraction. I command you to still do whatever you did to attract him (or her). If you've attracted him and he loves your hair, don't forget to do your hair. Don't be lazy. Don't let yourself go just because you're aging. Always work on presenting your best self. Yes, the human body changes over time, and we all know that. There's a huge difference between letting your body go (because you feel like you have someone) and your body going through a life change. As we age, our chromosomes die off, and that is why we obtain gray hairs. Our skin is meant to wrinkle as it loses its elasticity. We are meant to change, but we aren't meant to stop working on our health and appearances. I love that my grandparents still go on dates. They still dress up for each other, and they do their best to take care of each other.

See, it all comes full circle. This is why I mentioned health first, because a healthy relationship has to revolve around health. That sounds like a no-brainer, yet it is skipped often. If you want a healthy relationship, you need to focus on your health and the health of the other person. Physical fitness, eating well, emotional connectivity, and spiritual cleansing with your partner are needed to have an efficient relationship. It takes a multitude of skills, patience, and personal growth to be in an efficient relationship. This is why I scream at the top of my lungs when I see people who jump from relationship to relationship.

It's why I yell from the mountaintops that self-development, self-awareness, and introspection are necessary for the grand scheme of things. There are way too many people getting into relationships with the worst expectations, toxic behaviors, and mind-sets around them.

My friends, this is why I tell so many people not to force relationship conversations based on the "What are we?" question. There should never be a "What are we?" talk. That is something for the movies.

The real conversation should be based around these questions: "What are we going to do to increase our happiness today?" and "Where do we want to travel to, and how are we going to do it?" and "What do you want to improve, and how can I help you?"

To be in a relationship, marriage or committed, means that you're committing to giving this person the best of you, 180 percent of what you have. Now, if you're not even committed to giving yourself the best life you can give, how in the hell are you going to give that to another person? You will not. You will hurt her. Always commit to yourself; commit to him. Don't play the in-between game, because you can alleviate problems by working on the commitments.

Yes, being lonely can be a transformative state to sadness, but the real pain comes once you push away a person who loves you, because you didn't develop yourself enough. That's a special kind of hell that you don't want to deal with. I command you to push for self-development, for health, for fun, and for relationship conversations that build each other up. Then and only then will I agree with your fantasy-based claim that you deserve to be in a relationship. I will only agree once I see that you are building another person up—making her feel like she's a star—and growing daily to be the best person that you can be.

Yes, being lonely can be a transformative state to sadness, but the real pain comes once you push away a person who loves you, because you didn't develop yourself enough. That's a special kind of hell that you don't want to deal with. Always focus on growing so when you attract the right one, you are the right one.

– Sylvester McNutt III

Your commitment to each other should always be based around health. Simply sharing a journey of health together can transform any relationship. Both people should be concerned with keeping each other alive and well. No, you don't need stress and drama. You need laughter, good food, and commitment to each other's happiness. Focus on health:

mental, sexual, spiritual, and emotional.

—Sylvester McNutt III

Relationship Commitment

Relationship commitment is serious to this text and my teachings. I know everything about your soul, and you want this. You crave a love so deep that you reach a point of infiltration, where tectonic plates shift and mangle the earth's core. You want to feel loved, accepted, and cherished, and yes, you matter. However, the relationship entity will always have to become more important than you. Until you understand that, do not waste a single second claiming that you want a commitment. You are required to subtract all of your negative mind-sets and selfish ways before you get in a relationship. This is why the dating phase is so important. When you date, and date effectively, you can naturally grow into a selfless, serving couple. Dating effectively is the process of creating a prerelationship bubble built on trust, respect, and communication.

Dating is actually the most important phase because it gives you time to set up the ideologies for the relationship. If you do not do this, then you two will suffer and die in the shadows of each other's inadequacies. I command you to take this mind-set and to make it yours or make your own version that works for you, because it is the most efficient one you'll find in any text of this generation. Objectively, you'll find that this text puts you solely as the power. You have the power to create trust, respect, and open communication. If you do not do it, don't assume that anyone else will. You are the power. You are the source. You're reading this book, and you're the one obsessively thinking about your desire to have an effective relationship. If you've aligned with the text around commitment, then you need to understand that your soul is accepting it because it is resonating with this message on all levels. Commitment matters. Commitment is important because it guides our behaviors and gives us purpose and understanding.

Your vibrations are telling you that you are the one; you are the power; you are the pleasure and the reason that this next relationship will work. It's up to you to put every single ounce of your soul into it, every day, otherwise your commitment will be a fraud. Go get the love you want by being the love you want. In this generation, don't be afraid to love first, and never fear loving as deeply as you can. That is what the commitment is supposed to be about. It's all about you plunging into the unknown for results that may be unknown. In order to create the love, the life, and the environment that you want, don't ever be afraid to be it all first.

Go get the love

you want by

consistently

being the love

` you want.

—Sylvester McNutt III

The Past Is Not Real

I am going to ask you a few questions, and I want you to answer them aloud, as doing it like this is a transformative practice that helps with introspection:

> What did you eat for breakfast on January 11?
> What was your favorite food when you were fourteen years old?
> How many pairs of socks have you bought in your lifetime?

The more important question here is, who cares? Do we really care about the number of sock packages that you have purchased? Who cares what you ate for breakfast last week even?

The point is that too many men and women are living in the past and living their lives based on past actions. We're lacking the ability to be mindful. To be present is essential for happiness in your relationship. The truth is, we should all learn from past experiences, and we should have as many experiences as possible to develop well-rounded minds. But at no point should we allow these past experiences to influence us so strongly that they result in negative outcomes or attitudes for the present moments. A friend of mine once told me, "All guys have screwed me over before, so I don't trust them."

This is a girl who goes to bars to meet guys, so I said to her, "You don't trust guys, but the place you go to meet them is the bar, where your judgment and theirs is impaired because of alcohol. How could you possibly trust someone in that environment? Do you think there are better environments where you could meet someone?"

Her response was, "That's the only place to meet guys. But they're all dogs and liars; I don't trust them."

In her case, she is going to the bar with expectations of meeting a great guy. It's true; millions of good guys go to bars with the same hopes and aspirations of meeting someone great. However, with such a negative attitude, she is destined for failure because she is attracting the type of man who will "screw her over." She is giving herself a story and adding to her victim mind-set.

She does not realize that she is the narrator and the main actor in her story. I challenge you to see that you have a first- and third-person life. You can tap into the subjective and objective viewpoints of all of your situations; doing this will serve you a plate of happiness instead of a bowl of depression. Negative energy will only produce negative outcomes, the opposite of what she is looking for. I suggested to my friend that she try acting as if every guy she meets will have a chance to be her man. Act as if every single guy in the club has the potential to be the one.

She didn't like the idea. She said, "You're the logical one, and that's not logical."

I laughed and said, "Your logic, which you just stated, is that all guys are going to screw you over and that you're unwilling to feel anything positive about these men. There's no logical way you can negate my premise, which is to consider that every guy you meet has the potential to be the one. You're already doing one, and it's not working, so why wouldn't you try to other?"

She took a step back and realized that she'll never win a logical debate with me. She then laughed and said, "You know what, Sylvester? I actually don't like you right now. You make me think too much, but I get what you're saying, and I'll give it a try."

If you put aside everything that has happened to you and treat every person you meet like he (or she) actually has a chance to be the one, then you will empower him to behave naturally instead of trying to compete with others; this is especially true with men. Women are raised to fantasize and to think about weddings, dating, and partnership. Men are raised to think about success, strength, and sex. If you want a man to be the one, consider him for it; empower him to be it first. The same goes for women. Stop making it a challenge just to have a conversation with you. If you behave genuinely, you will attract a genuine person simply because you will vibrate with that frequency much more. If you are skeptical, jaded, and hateful, you have higher odds of meeting that type of person. We want higher odds—odds are about efficiency. The goal for this transformative thought is to create a plane of efficiency.

Clean Slate

One of the best things you can do in life is to give someone a clean slate upon meeting her or him. Do not discuss negative emotions or past experiences with a love interest too quickly. Instead, talk about the present moment. It is more important to trust each other and share experiences that feel good before the pain from the past comes up.

Of course we want the people we decide to share intimate details with to know everything about us, but the truth is, the most important things you need to know about each other are revealed the moment you decide you're interested—the present moment. It really makes no difference if you were *that* girl or guy in college who had *that* reputation. What happened before has nothing to do with anything. So before you seek to know all about a person's past or indulge in your story about the ex who did you oh so wrong, keep it to yourself, and concentrate on getting to know the person in front of you today. Start fresh; every person you meet will have shadows and demons. You're not entitled to know about what he or she did wrong in a relationship. People grow. People change and morph. If you seek the wrong information, you'll create an inefficient lane of distrust and confusion. People deserve a clean slate; you deserve a clean slate.

We all have skeletons in the closet, but I urge you to let them go. They hold no true value in this world. Once a person actually gets comfortable with you and starts to open up about the past, then it becomes another path to vulnerability. But in the beginning, this shouldn't be the focus. Give every lover and every situation a clean slate. Focus on the moment!The toxic, vile, and disgusting parts of your past need to be placed in one mental bag that you can drop off in a mental landfill. There's no reason to hold on to all that pain. It's stopping you from prospering. The negativity will pass, but you have to let go and allow it to pass. Don't hold on to the bag of negativity; drop it, and allow yourself to breathe.

Fear, Flaws, and Letting Go

Fear is my favorite subject in the world. The tagline on my website is the "Never Fear Effort Experience." I am obsessed with fear because, to me, fear represents the key to *life*. I believe that fear of judgment plagues a lot of people from being honest and open in a relational situation. Fear, from a neurobiological standpoint, generates from events associated with fear, known as the amygdala (a section in your brain). As we seek to understand fear, we must not be foolish to assume that we are capable of reaching a position where fear cannot exist. However, if we attempt to examine fear, we will notice that it is essential for human adaption to stress and emotional learning. Fear is anxiety that is psychological, physiological, and behavioral. It serves in animals and humans as recognition of a threat to well-being or survival. We have to be okay with and accept that fear is a part of our genetic makeup. The biology of the human body is fantastic, and the worse thing we can do is assign meaning to something that we have little to no knowledge of. We must accept that fear is normal and not describe it as good or bad, as both are relative and solely based on perception. I encourage you to just accept that fear is normal. The election of accepting that it is normal will allow you to not be held back by fear and your own assignment of it. We cannot allow fear to ruin our bid at love.

Everyone has fear, anxiety, and doubt. Do not let people like me fool you by our demeanor that we have it all together and that we do not struggle. The perception is that I am a confident speaker, and I walk with my head up high, but this is only perception. I too have things that I am scared of. The trick is not to allow fear to keep you away from opportunity and fulfillment. We are predisposed to fear; it is enmeshed in our DNA. We naturally focus on self-preservation— we will do anything in our power to make sure we survive. If something appears to threaten our survival, we will avoid, destroy, or manipulate the stimuli that causes the threat.

Do not walk around in fear, thinking you are the only one scared in life. People who suffer from anxiety often feel as if they're alone or they're the only ones feeling it. We all feel some type of anxiety, uneasiness, or discomfort. Especially when it comes to dating and love.

The way you overcome the anxiety is to understand everyone experiences it. You explore and find yourself, and you understand that nothing is more important than the present moment. Everyone has anxiety, fear, and doubt. That's normal—what will you do with it? Allow it to cripple you or accept that it's humane and acceptable? Your answer to that is transformative either way. We all have our areas of opportunities—most people will call them weaknesses, but I want you to erase that line from your script. There is no such thing as a weakness when we are talking about human beings. The other word that really bothers me is *flaw*. Who gets to determine flaws? And if there are so many flaws, show me the perfect people without flaws. Said person does not exist. Flaws are not real; thinking you have a flaw is illogical and will continue a state of suffering. I urge you to start using "area of opportunity." This phrase is a much more realistic look and is used in business. In fact, to look at a business model with efficiency, you would look at what it does well, but you would also consider the areas for opportunity. It makes sense that would then change the terminology to "area of opportunity."

As an entrepreneur, when I worked in sales management, and in my experience as an athlete, we measured areas of opportunity because the idea is to create a fine-tuned machine. Coaches, managers, and creators look at the "how" factor. How can we make attributes go up of things we don't do well? In some cases, you don't need to, because everything doesn't need to be developed. Tom Brady is a Super Bowl–winning quarterback and may likely go down as the greatest quarterback of all time—we don't know, but his résumé speaks for that type of conversation. If I were his coach, it would be egregious and reprehensible if I told this man that I want him to become a faster quarterback so he could run the ball more. That's illogical; it's not efficient; it's a slap in the face to the skills and talents he's mastered. Tom Brady indeed has become a master of accuracy, leadership, and clutch ability. He is so masterful at his craft that he has won several championships, which is the epitome of success in the NFL. This same analogy applies to us. Since I'm the writer here and you're the reader, you are Tom Brady. There are some things that you may be masterful at when it comes to your relationships. You may be very compassionate, understanding, and fun to be around. It's possible that you don't have the skill to be on time. It's possible that your partner really wants you to be on time, and for whatever reason, you just can't be on time.

As a coach and general manager of talent, you have to first accept each other, and then secondly, you mustn't harp over every little minuscule flaw, because there's no such thing. Yes, you could be on time, but you treat me so well it feels like we're winning championships every day. If we both feel like we are winning championships, then why do we need to nitpick at our areas of opportunities? Be aware of it, but don't harp on it, especially when things are going well. At this point, your love awakening has occurred, and you're starting to see things in a different light—you're ready to let go of the past because you see that it is nothing but a story. You subtract the assignment of fear. You understand that nothing is promised and that fear is normal, but it won't hold you back. As far as your consciousness and awareness is concerned, you've already opened up a new, transformative state. Now your soul is ready for skills and strategies.

Chapter 3

Skills and Strategies

for Efficient Love

Trust: The First Pillar of Efficient Relationship Building

I have identified three main pillars that need to be focused on, watered, nourished, and placed on a clean-slate platform to build a majestic relationship on. If you want to have an efficient relationship, one that is abundant in togetherness, love, and growth, I encourage you to focus on building these pillars: trust, respect, and communication. If your present relationship is suffering, I encourage you to examine and introspect where these pillars currently are at and then find ways to implement new ideologies and behaviors into them that will garner you a new outcome.

The first pillar is trust, and yes, I feel like it's important to understand trust should be the primary function. All actions develop off of trust or distrust. It's imperative that you go into interactions understanding that the goal should be to find ways to build trust. Each situation is different. This isn't something that should be forceful, and it's actually the hardest to do because to become a trusting person requires a certain level of self-power and self-awareness that a lot of people lack.

In this section I have a few guiding principles that are realistic, reasonable, and necessary that you should implement immediately into your ideology of trust. I also challenge one of the most famous quotes and show you how it isn't logical. Let's dive in.

Build Trust

When we think about the process of building, we think of something that takes time and that is partial. If you want to build a brick wall outside of your house to display your paintings, but you're not a bricklayer and don't understand the process, you would have to start off small, right? Let's assume that we are all bricklayers when it comes to love and dating. When you meet a new person, you don't trust him or her; in fact, we live in a world that is full of distrust and deceit. As a result, we're not even starting at the ground level. We're starting with a deficiency. Since that's the case, picture yourself standing there, outside of your house, looking at a hole in the ground and the bricks in one pile, with no wall built. However, you're aware of the fact that you need and want this wall, but you don't know how, and you're in the hole, literally. This is the way we walk around now. You may have your walls up, and your heart may be guarded. I'll never tell you not to guard yourself and protect yourself. I will tell you that excessive guarding can cause you to practice sheltering yourself. You're conditioning yourself to feel like staying sheltered and guarded is normal, but one of the key components of trust is vulnerability.

Vulnerability—Trust will transform your relationship for the better; a lack of trust will destroy your relationship. Those are axioms. There is no gray area with trust. It's on or off. You don't kind of trust someone; you either do or you don't. Trust also varies based on the event or situation. For example, I may trust you to make a good meal, but I don't trust you to run my bathwater, because you run it too hot. I may trust you to do laundry, but I may not trust the way you drive. Those are different types of trust. They are really just lifestyle preferences, and although one could argue that they reflect trust, ultimately, they have nothing to do with what we're exploring here and are trivial.

Vulnerability is the ability to reveal your true self, your scars and pain. The ability to show a stranger or a loved one the inner workings of your essence. Is it hard? Yes, actually—for some it's impossible because we don't want to feel shame or unworthy. Again, at first, nobody needs to know about your trauma. In the very beginning it should be about fun, conversation, and getting to know this new person. As time goes on, it is imperative that you practice vulnerability, especially once you get into any committed relationship. The other person needs to have a high awareness and understanding into your thoughts, feelings, and ideas.

Vulnerability has a neurobiological connection to improving all relationships and love. It is your goal, mission, and right to desire a path of vulnerability. A state of vulnerability pushes the user to connect. Connection links to trust, love, belonging, and spiritual growth. Vulnerability is not comfortable, but it's necessary. The part that hurts us most is the perception that we can control our outcomes by obsessively picking out and manipulating every little detail about our environments. We can't, however. Texts like *Dear Love Life* give you the power to control your effort, efficiency, and productivity in the equations that create your outcomes, but to expect to control the entire environment or another person is unrealistic and will cause you a great deal of suffering. Life is a street fight—you're going to get punched, kicked, and stabbed a little, and that's realistic. In order to develop trust, you have to be willing to be okay with trauma. In order for your relationship to work, you have to develop trust. As a chain of cause and effect, you need to be okay with trauma to accept the idea of being in love and creating or sustaining a relationship. That is the ironic part of it all. We literally have to be okay with relationship murder, with betrayal, and with becoming devastated. In order to be ready for a relationship, you have to be willing to deal with those possibilities. But how? How does one get there? Through preparation. Devouring texts like this is preparation. One has to practice the art of being vulnerable. Once you can find the behaviors of practicing vulnerability, then and only then do you create the lanes for trust.

True or False: Trust Takes Time—Abolish the mind-set that trust takes time, and implement this new one: trust is about consistent investment. It's safe to say that most people want to feel safe in a relationship.

We want commitments and titles because they make us feel safe. That safety is illusionary at best because there are no promises or guarantees in relationships. We all know or have been in situations where people act like they love you to your face, but their actions, behind your back, show that they're everything but what they claimed to be. That's not sad. It's just realistic. We've seen these situations, and expecting a verbal guarantee to prevent these actions is juvenile and egregious. With trust, you actually don't need the measurement of time. There are people who have been married for twenty years, and they don't trust each other. That situation is more common than we'd like to admit, and it's not because marriage and commitment are bad ideas. It's because people get into these situations without awareness, without skill, and without understanding what they're doing. People in relationships who lack trust still stay in the relationships, and they suffer through it. Some people will tell you that being in a relationship is about suffering through with people. I beg to differ. I don't deserve to just suffer through any level or format of life, casually and complacently. Do you? If we're not being efficient, then I have to ask, what the hell are we doing? Once your awareness allows you to see that relationships are about skills, skill development, and practice, then you understand that this is a competitive sport and not just a poem of fantasy. Trust doesn't need time. Trust is an amalgamation of the raw investment you put in plus your own level of emotional health. Trust is about your perception and view of the world. Do you view it like this—people have to prove that they're trustworthy over a certain amount of time? That's not efficient or logical based on the examples above. Instead, the new philosophy on trust is blind trust.

Blind Trust

My three-year-old goddaughter trusts her mother and father to feed her, to keep her safe, and to entertain her every single day. If you walk up to her, will she trust you? No, but she won't distrust you. She will invest in having a conversation with you. She will invest in sharing her food or play space with you. She will not have distrust for you until you show that you are not trustworthy. Maybe you startle her, eat her food, or act violent toward her. The trust that a toddler has, which is normal human nature, is the trust we need to develop efficient relationships. As we go through life, we go through traumatic experiences, and we don't heal. We internalize and harvest the pain. We go through a process called *classical conditioning*. No matter what you think you know or don't actually know, you've experienced or are experiencing classical conditioning. My goddaughter likes to watch videos of volcanoes with me. We only watch these videos on my Xbox at my apartment. When she sees the light and hears the sound of my Xbox, she says, "Uncle Sly, I'm so ready to watch volcanoes." She's associated the audio and visual stimuli as her brain signals to expect that we will watch volcanoes. This is classical conditioning.

Watching Volcanoes (Uncontrolled Stimulus— UCS)

My Goddaughter (Unconditioned Response— UCR)

When we use the word *conditioning*, we are always referring to learning. If I say that I am conditioning myself to become a better husband, it means that I am learning how. To label it uncontrolled and unconditioned means that it is natural and normal, without force. The Xbox lights going on and clicking is called a neutral stimulus (NS). It tells the UCR that the UCS will occur. So in my example, the Xbox tells my goddaughter that it's time to watch volcanoes. The NS had to be learned—she's seen it on before, and she's seen me and her father play video games. She eventually learned that the Xbox can play volcano videos, and that brings her a great deal of excitement. She was conditioned to hear and see the Xbox and then to watch videos of volcanoes. That is called a trial. Once the UCS and UCR are paired together, then you establish classical conditioning. Once the Xbox itself started to solicit the excitement feeling from her, then the Xbox became a conditioned stimulus (CS), and she became a conditioned response (CR). She now reacts once the Xbox comes on, and of course I feel a certain level of obligation to watch a video with her even if my intention was to play music.

Classical conditioning is the reason for a lot of suffering in relationships. It's the main reason why people who have trusted and lost trust maneuver through life unwilling to give the blind trust needed to be efficient; they continue to suffer. They internalize the pain because it has been learned from a previous situation in the current relationship or because a previous relationship has caused them to distrust—they have learned they shouldn't trust people. If you are one of these people, you will suffer, and you will cause a great deal of suffering to another person unless one condition is met. Unless the person you're with feels the exact same way as you.

We talked about confirmation biases earlier. If your partner confirms your ideologies and inefficient perceptions on trust, the relationship may work. This generation is broken because we don't understand or learn psychology early on. After reading this, you'll have an advantage in dating. Dating is a competitive game. This lesson here is on trust. It's imperative that you develop trust by giving blind trust to people from day one. Your goal shouldn't be to force a person through years and years of proving trust. It doesn't take time. Trust takes raw investment; trust takes both people giving the other person a clean slate. Trust is about trusting blindly, like a child trusts and believes in his or her parents. Trust is about unlearning the things that are keeping you trapped inside the illusion of "trust takes time." Yes, time is an element, but it's not the most important element. Trust is deeper than that, and now you see that trust is the lifeline for your relationship. I hope you cherish it now, tomorrow, and forever.

You should be having conversations about trust from the beginning. Always remember that if you do not develop trust, you increase the ability to create deficient relationships. If you develop trust, you increase your ability to develop effective relationships. Those are axioms. If you're in a relationship without trust, the first step is to acknowledge and talk about it. Do not be offensive or defensive. Talk objectively about it with your partner. Talk about why you both feel it is important and ways that you could improve the trust levels. Refer back to the classical conditioning information given, and introspect your situation. You could easily solve most problems by finding a way to figure them out. Without trust, you're just two people playing house, having survivor-series sex, and fighting, arguing, and grappling for position because you don't know how to hold on to each other. You're manipulating and ruining each other's ability to become conditioned to something efficient.

It's imperative that you each focus on letting go of what impacted you in the past. If you do not analyze what you've been classically conditioned to, you will repeat the same steps of mistrust. Just because one person did something to you does not means that another person will. That type of logic is not valid. Each person has his or her own set of motivations, skills, and behaviors. Don't ever be someone who publically claims that you want love from a man or woman, but on the other end you're screaming about how there are no good men or women. Don't be this type of person, because you are the most confused, conflicted, and delusional person to date. Take the time you need to heal and grow from the trauma. It's nobody's responsibility to heal your heart. Nobody should suffer because you don't know how to heal. That's not fair. Continue to grow. Focus on trust. It will save you years of pain and heartache. Focusing on trust will give you years of happiness, bliss, and nirvana in relationships. You deserve that, right?

Breach of Trust

There's a common theme that is going on in our generation, and it revolves around privacy, entitlement, and cell phones. I define a breach of trust as a direct violation of the relationship agreements and any behavior that can be detrimental toward the ability to build trust. Following are some examples.

Cell Phone Investigation—Investigations occur across the world by police, governments, and insecure lovers daily. Typically investigations are cold, calculated, and uncomfortable. There's nothing pleasurable, glamorous, or exhilarating about an interrogation. When the police conduct investigations, they are looking to place blame for a crime on someone, and your information will either help free you or help point them in the direction of the perpetrator. If the police investigate you, you will feel like you're walking on eggshells because you don't want to say the wrong thing. You don't want to do something that will show your guilt or participation in a crime. If, in fact, you're not guilty and they manipulate you into trying to confess, you'll resent and despise the police. If you are 100 percent innocent in a relationship setting and you get accused of something, a few events will happen. You'll feel defensive, confused, and protective of yourself. You'll immediately want this person, group, or entity to go away. You will not want to be your natural self; you'll push them away, because they don't trust you. That creates resentment and destroys trust. From a stranger or authority figure, we observe that these behaviors push us away from them, thus setting up avenues of inefficient behaviors and ruined relationships. How does it make you feel if your lover interrogates you? How does it make you feel if you have to walk on eggshells just so a person who claims to love you can complete an interrogation of you? Do you deserve to be interrogated in your relationship? I certainly don't, nor will I settle for that type of torture chamber.

Some people believe that delving into another person's phone, laptop, or personal journals are allowed since they're in relationships with them. Realistically, you don't control any person on this planet. You should not be trying to control adults. Hell, I'm an international best-selling author, and I'm aware that all I can do is present information. It's up to you to see the value in it, to introspect, and to grow. Just like it's up to you to give your partner the freedom and trust that person needs to make decisions. If you try to control every little aspect about your lover, the real question is, how do you expect them to grow into a loving being?

I Went Through His/Her Phone, and I Found Something—No matter what you find, please understand that you committed a breach of trust. Every person is allowed and deserves to have freedom and space. Would you go through your best friend's phone searching for things? Probably not. In fact, I have both male and female best friends, and I've never seen any of their phones in over ten years. They haven't checked my phone either. My cell phone, computer, and journal contain personal data. But you found something on his (or her) phone, and now what? Remember the term I introduced earlier called *confirmation bias*? Confirmation bias is another element that destroys or builds relationships. In most situations, what I see is people blow out of proportion what they find in order to overcredit their own confirmation biases and intuition instincts. Other times, I see people connect dots that don't even go together. The entire act is disrespectful, egregious, and wrong. If the person did something wrong and broke your trust, and then you checked his phone to discover that he is untrustworthy, I just have one question: How long can this entanglement last in an efficient, healthy way if both people are committing a breach of trust? After back-to-back breaches, how the hell is anyone going to feel safe or secure?

Imagine you are living in an underground bunker because there is an extinction-level event. Fast-forward. A few weeks later you have two break-ins and breaches on the exterior. They take water, clothing, and bathing items. You would become infuriated because they're taking away from your resources. At this point, you're on high alert.

If you put your relationship on high alert because of breaches of trust, how is it supposed to last? In the imaginary bunker, they took water, food, and supplies, but in your relationship, you give away trust, which is the fallout-shelter equivalent. You ruin it. Eventually the situation gets uptight and hostile as both parties try to manipulate and gain leverage on the other. Trust is the most fragile and finite resource in your relationship. In a lot of situations, once it's gone, it's gone forever. Once there's one breach of trust, it opens up the floodgates for more and more. In my mind, there's always a chance to recover and grow from differences, but the average person does not have the skill to succumb to these pressures. You cannot commit a breach of trust and then validate it because of the data you've found. That's actually not logical. What happens when you search a phone and find nothing? Where do we draw the line on right or wrong?

If you try to use this logic in your defense, I want you to understand that you're manipulating the situation to your benefit and gain. People who manipulate and control situations for their own personal gains and advancements, with a lack of concern for others' rights and well-being, are referred to as sociopaths. You could be bordering on sociopathic behavior via manipulation and control if you think it's okay for your victim, which is the person you're dating, to be subjected to your investigations. Sociopaths have a heightened sense of entitlement. A sociopathic person says things like, "Well, I'm having sex with her, so I deserve to see her phone" or "I have the right to go through his phone because my intuition was telling me that something is off." Sociopaths are secretive, paranoid, and authoritarian, and they rationalize the pain they inflict on others.

This is not a joking matter anymore. We are well aware of the videos on social media that poke fun of the behavior of insecure and controlling women. However, in the incident of breaching trust in order to gain leverage of information, we're learning that it's much more devastating than we realize and is no laughing matter. Some of this introspection is alluding to possibilities of identifying sociopathic behavior. That is an experience that nobody wants to deal with.

My Intuition Told Me to Check His/ Her Phone—False. Your intuition told you that you have a feeling that needs to be introspected. Your intuition is an intrinsically occurring event. You do not need to seek external validation for something that is occurring deep inside of you. Your intuition told you to talk, and your insecure, sociopathic ways told you that it was okay to lurk behind this person because of two reasons. One, your partner won't find out, and it'll appease your need for information. Two, it'll give you the ammo you need if you find something worth fighting or breaking up over. Again, this behavior isn't gender specific. We often use the word *intuition* and refer to it as solely a woman's ability. Intuition is a human trait. I don't want this text to come off as if I am attacking women's intuition, because this isn't a gender-specific behavior. It's a generational behavior that has to stop immediately.

The next time your intuition signals something that makes you uneasy or unsure in the relationship, I don't want you to ignore it. I want you to use more efficient behaviors to attack it. Once you learn the efficient skills, it's easy to have an action plan for the stress and problems. Next time, go create an open-ended conversation, not an interrogation. Don't seek any expectation other than to be open and to communicate. You'll have to be vulnerable and risk creating the conflict of what you feel, unless one condition is met. If you have the skill to deal with the uneasy feeling on your own, then and only then do not bring it up. Most people need reassurance and understanding to make those uneasy feelings go away. Simple communication can resolve them, but please understand the conversation and everything the other person says are external solutions to internal problems. Ultimately, it's all up to you to correct this suffering by whatever means seem efficient.

Talking, introspecting, or just waiting it out.

Intuition Awareness: Don't ever ignore your intuition; it's usually correct. But just because you're usually correct doesn't mean you're always correct. There's an interesting relationship that intuition has with assumptions. It's wise of us to develop efficient skills in order to reduce the risk of making assumptions based on insecurities. If your partner cheated on you and the majority of the dirt was done behind a cell phone, it's possible, because of classical conditioning, that you'll assume all of the future occurrences related to the cell phone will be unpleasant ones. It's necessary, in cases like this, that we recondition the brain so that the stimulus does not directly correlate to pain or distrust. This can take time. It will take work. It might take a change of environment, scenery, and even people, but becoming aware of it is necessary because trust is fragile.

How to Get Trust Back after It's Gone

The consciousness of this society is confusing. At times it feels as if there is a steady decline of rational sense and morality. At other times it feels as if we are joining, combing, and uniting to make the human experience a more efficient and enjoyable one. For the life of me I cannot figure out why we still use plastic bags in grocery stores, why we're in a system that forces us to work forty hours per week, and why we still have racism and sexism. There are logical answers and levels of introspection that we could explore for those questions, but that's not this book. I just don't understand why these things go on. Just like, why does it feel like there's an increase in cheating, relationship backstabbing, and the decline of healthy relationships? I was asked a question at one of my speaking engagements this year, and I still do not think there will ever be a solid, tangible answer. The question is something that I still think about to this day: Because of the media and self-expression, are we seeing more problems with awareness, relationships, and such, or have the problems always been there, and now they just have a platform?

First, every society deals with problems because there's always something that is set in place that isn't efficient. We don't know the answer. I can tell you this—I was around and dated before cell phones were popular, and it felt genuine and real. Now people will rationalize not talking to you on a date, while they update their Snapchat and scroll their news feed right in front of you. Like I've stated, social media and cell phones are tools. Tools needs to be used appropriately in order to be effective. You wouldn't cut your vegetables up with a hammer, and you wouldn't put a nail in the wall using a knife. Could you? Sure, but would you? Probably not. That's the difference between possibility and probability. It's highly possible and probable that if you're dating or creating a relationship in or after the year 2016, you will run into issues where trust may have been broken or breached. So the next question plaguing most relationships is, how do we get it back? How do we get it back, especially knowing, from this text, that trust is one of the most important pillars of efficient success for the relationship? Here are a few steps and principles to help you regain and rebuild trust after it has been broken:

1. **Accountability and Admittance**: In most cases, nobody is going to leave. If you're having conversations about what happened and why, then that means both of you are trying to rationalize the root cause and outcome. That's actually the key to rebuilding trust after an incident. I suggest that you limit how much detail you offer. It's too trivial and distracting to worry about all of the finite details of what happened. Oftentimes, people feel bad, so they tell their partners every little

detail, and this creates too many bridges to overcome. Honestly, if you ever get in a situation where trust has diminished, don't chase every little detail. Focus on the root cause so it can be addressed and so the two can move forward from it. The focus should be on asking, why did it happen in the first place and how do we prevent this? Oftentimes I've seen situations where the details actually implant and nourish insecurities inside the victims. Those insecurities then become the main issues that the relationships suffer in the future. If you are ever a victim of distrust, I urge you not seek the details of the event. They'll hurt you more in the long run. If you are the one that created the distrust via an action, it is imperative that you enter a full state of accountability and admittance. You hurt someone already, so this is your time to be brutally honest. Telling more lies here will always make the situation worse. Breach of trust plus a lie is the number one way to push away trust and the other person.

2. **What Is Missing**: There is something missing. What is it? Have you talked about it? Has your sex life changed? Has

the communication changed? Has the desire changed? Are you talking to someone new, and it's conflicting you? No matter what, it is imperative that both parties go on a journey of introspection. They need to figure out what they're not doing that they used to do. When the dynamics of a relationship change, it's imperative that we understand the smallest changes can have the biggest impact. In the last point I talked about how important it is to be honest. This is what you have to be honest about. It's imperative that you're honest with what is missing, because partners can't work on something if they don't know about it.

3. **Transparency**: The ability to be liquid, to be fluid and see-through. The ability to have no shadows or closed doors that will prevent communication. The ability to let go of judgment, fear, and insecurity in an effort to reveal your true self. Changing the relationship rules and having the willingness to remove passwords and screen locks. Having the ability to share cell phones, to (on command) show e-mails, social media, and personal data. Earlier, I mentioned how scary it is to respect the other

person's space and to not invade his (or her) privacy. However, after a breach of trust, the other person is looking for closure from the trauma and reassurance that his or her partner will not exhibit this same behavior again—the closure that only comes with help from a partner. After trust has been broken, the person who was hurt will be looking for the other person to show that his or her behavior has changed. That is the only way to break the classical conditioning. Changed behavior takes time, new skills, and a different level of consciousness; this takes time. It's the only way to change the classical conditioning and to relearn a new path for the brain waves. Will it have to be like that every day and forever? It's possible that it will, but it is not probable.

4. **A Formal, Written Apology**: If you cheat or just break trust, and you want this person back, you need to take the most genuine step you can. Sure, you can hold her and talk to her, but I want you to write a letter. Make it something tangible that she can have. This letter serves two purposes actually. It is you taking accountability and telling her exactly how things will go in the future. This letter is

also your way of keeping yourself accountable. It has been proven that writing down goals actually improves the efficiency level in workers, athletes, and relationships. In this letter, put a clause that says once you guys build trust up, you will celebrate by burning the letter together. It will be a party of trust. This way, both people are agreeing that they are working toward trust together. It cannot be a lopsided, one-person event. If you messed up, she has to forgive you, and she has to agree to work with you to recover. If you committed the breach, you have to be prepared to understand that this is a process.

5. **Let That Shit Go**: The person who was cheated on, the victim, actually holds the most amount of power here. He has to measure if he wants to leave the relationship or not. He overobsesses about if he'll be able to trust her again. He'll have to consider dealing with a public breakup. Nobody wants a public breakup. In this generation, most couples have their relationships online, and for him to stop posting pictures of her or to announce the breakup would bring shame and embarrassment. After all of the

scenarios play out, the best thing you can do is let that shit go. You're staying in the relationship, right? Okay, then do your best to let it go. Be present; let it go as quickly as you can.

How to Stop Cheating

There is a lack of perspective on this topic. We as humans just jump on these people and provide the negativity, instead of support and perspective. I hope *Dear Love Life* provides some valuable perspective on How to Stop Cheating. Nobody cares about the people who cheat. We just black label them and tell them how they're bad people. We don't look at their upbringings, environments, or skill sets. How is that helpful? It's critical and selfish of us to be so mean toward this population of people. Remember, *how to be in a relationship* is not a class in school. We basically have to live life, watch our parents, and destroy our hearts over and over until we get it. It's imperative that we always remain objective and understand others' positions—that's called empathy. *Every* person will face temptation in a relationship. It's inevitable. This section serves two purpose: First, it will help those people who consistently cheat and need advice on how to stop, and it is judgment free. Second, this section will plant the seeds for a younger generation who will for sure need guidance and who *will* face temptation. This is a preventative section. Take notes; keep an open mind. Every step may not work for you depending on where you are, but apply the ones that do.

1. Represent Your Relationship Online if You Represent Your Life Online Too

My friend Marcus Jennings is a yoga instructor superstar from Chicago, Illinois. Currently, he lives in Nashville, Tennessee, and travels the world teaching yoga, spreading light and love. I've learned something from him that is extremely important. He has been married for well over a decade and has a huge following online. His social network footprint is well over one hundred thousand people. His posts consists of yoga flows, yoga poses, and information to help followers increase their yoga practices. However, once a week, he posts his wife as his woman-crush Wednesday post. On Instagram, that is a procedure for a man to show love and validation to the woman he cares about or the woman he has a crush on. Some men will post celebrities because they feel like there is no harm in it. Some never post their girls or wives because they like to keep their relationships private. Some people just really aren't into the Internet like that, so they might not even know what Instagram is. Let's be honest—we all have at least one online profile.

My belief is that if your profile represents you—you post pictures of yourself, your life, and your interests, then that is what I call a *personal page*. If your page is anonymous and you just post random quotes, your name isn't on it, and you just share things that have nothing to do with your life, I call that a *ghost page*. Believe it or not, there's a lot of people who aren't concerned with creating or sharing content, but they do like to log on to social media and just look at content. I call them ghosts because you really don't know much about what they're doing. Then you have pages like mine. I'm a writer, so most of my posts pertain to my writing. I have an online store, and I sell products. I call this a *branded page*. If needed, please review the three. I'll actually speak on these later: branded, personal, and ghost. They serve different functions for the online sphere, and users can change from one to the other at any given time, but they can't be all three at the same time.

If you have a ghost page, I hardly think you'll put your relationship on it, because you literally don't post anything on there. From my observation of being an online content creator and running a business/blog online for the last four years, I would say that this is about 20 percent of the accounts that I see.

Brands are tricky. Some brands cause you to interact with people, which is a slippery slope. For example, you might be a barber, a personal trainer, or a traveling yoga instructor. These are brands that cause you to be around people, even if you're building the brand using an online model. In this case, I find it necessary and essential that you share the component of your relationship.

Obviously, there are so many levels to this. If it's a brand-new arrangement and you guys are still dating, I think we can all understand why you wouldn't want to share that relationship. It's too new, and that's fair. If it's your marriage or a long-term relationship, we definitely can see why you would share it online. It would make sense then. At that point, your relationship truly is a part of your life, and it's nothing worth hiding. The branded people are not off the hook. I implore you to consider sharing your relationship online. In fact, here's a small excerpt of a conversation that I had with

Marcus Jennings, the yoga teacher.

Sylvester: Why do you post your wife on your page every week?

Marcus: My Instagram page belongs to me and my wife. I'm not going to act single online. I don't care if it makes my business better. I love my wife and my marriage is a big part of my life. I don't post out of obligation. I post her because I like seeing her on my page.

– Conversation between. @SylvesterMcNutt & @SuperHumanYogi

This section is on building trust. If we want to build trust, we have to consistently do actions that revolve around building trust. Representing your relationship online, in a space where you represent your life, makes perfect sense. Now, there are people who truly believe in keeping all of the details about their relationships private, and I respect that too. In this landscape of dishonest, disloyal, and deceitful people, it makes sense that some want to protect their relationships from the masses. I truly believe that being open about it and showing it *helps* a person stay committed and faithful. The majority of us want to match our online profiles. Some of us do a little too much and go too far, and we stretch the truth a little bit. I believe the majority of us are good people, and we're just sharing what we like. For those people it will actually help you if you see yourself online, being committed. It's like watching yourself on Netflix. You actually want your character to win, to thrive, to be the best he can be.

Putting your relationship online, as long as it's a solid one that you both believe in, will ease pressure and give more confidence to the relationship. People can say that "It's just social media," but I'll never accept that response, because it's not logical. If it was "just" anything, you wouldn't be using it, because "just" is implying that it's a miniscule and unimportant adventure. If that's the case, why in the hell are you online with an active profile? Couldn't you just be building a business, in the gym, or focusing on making more money for yourself? Don't ever try to tell me or anyone that it is "just" social media, and don't let anyone try to tell you that either. People use that line as an excuse to justify their shitty behavior. The buck stops here. I don't care if you have one or one million followers, share the relationship that you claim is important to you, especially if you're sharing other things that you feel like are important to you. If it's just social media, then it's just one post about your life, so share it. See. That "just" logic doesn't stand up. I have to be real and honest. I see this behavior a lot more from men than I do women. I am a man. I understand. Here's how men think: *These women are haters, and I don't want these dudes trying to get in my business. I don't want anyone to mess up what I have with her, especially while I am building it.* I agree and feel the same way. I've always felt like that. In fact, I've never really been the one to share my relationship online, but I'll tell you why I do it: for her.

Fellas, if you're struggling with the reasons of why you should do it, just do it for her. We will never understand the feelings she gets when she is publically claimed by the man she cares about. It might be just Instagram or just Facebook. Just put the post up so your woman will be happy.

The Reversal: No man is required to post his relationship online, no matter what this text or any other text implies. At the end of the day, he is still allowed to have free will and free range to run his social media accounts however he wishes. The women I interviewed said they felt inclined to post online just out of respect for the relationships. Men like Marcus Jennings are the rare ones who feel inclined to share their relationships online. This is a new phenomenon because of the new tools we have: social media, cell phones, and texting. This is about respect, communication, and understanding. At no point should he feel forced or coerced to share something that is so intimate to him. We see images of Stephen Curry, his wife, and his daughter all over the Internet, daily. However, we never see images of Justin Timberlake, his wife, and his kid. One is not better than the other. Both are entitled to carry on how they wish. We don't know, but I'm guessing they both have enjoyable relationships. It's important to be empathic to the fact that we all have different love lives and different values, and some truly enjoy being private with their personal matters, and that's okay.

As a woman, you have to have confidence, security, and belief in yourself and your relationship. You have to know your man and his style. If he is the private type, it is unfair and damaging of you to press him into posting things online. You have to trust, uplift, and respect your man to be as he is. As a man, consider doing it because it'll help her believe that the end of the pie tastes good too.

It is important that people become aware of this too: cell phones and social media didn't really boom until about 2010. This means that there are people who grew up dating without cell phones, without social media, and without the instant access to hundreds of people. The younger generations have grown up with cell phones, social media, and other options. It's important to understand that each person's generation has different mind-sets and value systems. If you go out to a bar with a bunch of twenty somethings, you'll see that damn near all of them will be on their phones. Girls hardly engage fully. They just look disinterested and stay on Snapchat all night. I urge everyone to really evaluate who you are with and your relationship to social media. Some don't care, some need it, and others just allow it to distract them.

In conclusion, the pronouns could be switched, it could be her who is hiding and he who is posting. Just talk about it, from the beginning. Bring it up so you both know what you're getting yourself into and then *accept* and *respect* your partner's decision.

Posting your relationship online may help both parties stay more committed, more invested into growing; you will want to give more and not cheat. Nobody wants to do a public breakup, because those are not fun at all. Yes, that adds pressure to the relationship, but depending on who you are, it may add support. You may have friends, family, and even online friends who support you. Support is real and contagious.

Protect what you care about.
Honor your commitments.
Build yourself,
your partner,
and relationship entity up,
always.
Eliminate everything that
attempts to destroy your
relationship.

—Sylvester McNutt III, *Dear Love Life*

If there's no trust, it's just two people playing house.

Trust is the safe haven that keeps the two bonded.

Be a genuine, kind, and trustworthy person.

Look at your relationship like it is an entity bigger and greater than you; both partners are contributors and need to value the pillar of trust.

Trust is the backbone to efficient relationships.

—Sylvester McNutt III, *Dear Love Life*

2. Stop Putting Yourself in Inefficient Situations

I am a man. This is simple. We like sex. We like attractive women. This never changes. When you commit to one woman, it does not go away. One of the keys to your success as a man (or a woman) is to stop putting yourself in inefficient situations. I literally will say to myself, "I cannot put myself in this dumbass situation." It's not appropriate to go to the bars and clubs with your friends who chase sex and create sexually charged situations. Can you do it? Yes, you can. Is it efficient? In most cases, it is not. There's no reason to do anything that is going to violate the relationship's chance of growing into something magical. In some cases, you have to cut off certain friendships.

Building a relationship is about creating one unit, one team, synching up to be one heartbeat and union. It's vital that some people are left out. In some cases, we can remain friends with people we were once in love with, people we used to have sexual interactions with, or people who were just missed connections. If you truly can be friends with those people, that means they respect your relationship. They support it. They can be present with you, your lover, and all of the baggage that comes with you two. *In* most cases, that is impossible. If you can't bring them around your lover, then what would be the point of maintaining secret relationships? A secret relationship such as this goes against everything I have been teaching. It is not going to build trust. It is literally going to create insecurity and doubt. Even the most secure and strongest person is going to ask, internally, "Am I not good enough?" or "Do they want to get back with this person?" or "Are they going to leave me while they work on their friendship?" These are all valid and fair thoughts.

I'm one of the most confident people on the planet, but if my woman was hell bent on managing friendships with a man who hurt her, caused her pain, and used her, I wouldn't feel right. If I am doing my best, giving her love and attention and taking care of every need that I can, and yet she still went back to her lover while staying in a relationship with me, it would raise concerns. Especially if they were not friends when we met. It really makes a person go into a spiral of uncontrollable overthinking and overanalyzing. Nobody likes to deal with loss; in fact, it is human nature to stay in a toxic situation because we naturally think we can improve it. We do not want to deal with loss. Loss brings feelings of abandonment, unworthiness, and depression. This is why people stay. Please don't put people through this emotional roller coaster of confusion. Nobody can control who you decide to be friends with, but think about who you say "I love you" to. Think about the person you lay next to every night. Think about the person who hasn't even put you through all of the pain that the other person did. In some cases, you go back to and try to remain with your ex for one reason and one reason only: Stockholm syndrome.

Some of you are so wrapped up in the narcissistic mind control your ex has over you that you don't even realize that you're a victim of Stockholm syndrome. When a victim has empathy and concern for the captor or person oppressing her (or him), she can align, feel bad for, and fall victim to his brainwashing. You may think that you want to be friends with your ex, but if he's not respecting your relationship or using any emotional influence to sway you, you are trapped. The victim often feels a sort of confusion, especially since she is partially dependent on the oppressor. This happens in abusive relationships, bank robberies, child abuse, or in a situation where you think that you love your ex, but such exes are really just oppressors. An oppressor does not care about you. He only cares about what you can do for him, how he can control you, and how he can manipulate you to act out of control. He wants you to think irrationally so you can rationalize doing things that are irrational.

If you've started a new relationship, leave this fucking person alone. He will ruin it, because once the new person finds out that you still want your ex, it will instantly break trust. This entire book, thus far, has been giving ways to build trust. If you want the new relationship to last, you have to cut this oppressor off or suffer and watch your relationship crumble. These are your choices, but only you know what is best. I highly recommend that you make your partner feel comfortable. If you go back to a person who has already shown she (or he) can live without you, guess what she'll do? She'll oppress you and then kick you to the curb when she's done with you. She doesn't want or need you, and you have a person who wants you. Make your current partner comfortable, and eliminate the situation.

This is called emotional cheating. In my opinion, it's worse than physical cheating. (Physical cheating may be a harder thing for some women to deal with.) Keep in mind that I am a male. We talked about sex in the last chapter. Men don't feel the emotions that women have when they have sex. For me, if she's emotionally cheating, it will be very hard to want to continue anything with her, especially because as a man, I don't naturally get to show my true emotions. Be very, very careful with this situation. The solution is to stop putting yourself in these situations. You have to make a decision and stick to it. Otherwise you will break everyone involved.

3. Talk about What Is Missing

I believe with all of my heart that this is the number one reason why people cheat. I believe that people evaluate what they're receiving versus what they want, which is based on their value system, and they cheat because they need what they're not getting. It's really just another objective view of causation, if you really think about it. If there's no sex and a person cheats, it makes sense. He (or she) cheated because he wanted sex and didn't feel like going through the stress of fighting a person who is withholding sex from him. This makes sense logically. In emotionally cheating, it's pretty apparent that the reason you're cheating is because you don't feel comfortable with the other person. You don't want to share that vulnerability piece with him (or her). You don't feel like you can open up and be yourself, so you go find a new conversation with a new friend because bottling in how you feel is pure suffering. If you ever feel like this, it means you need to go have a conversation with your lover, now. If he doesn't seem to hear you or doesn't express enough concern, you need to take an extreme measure. Maybe unplug all of the technology in the house. Maybe write a letter. Maybe you set up a date to discuss this. Only you know what is extreme for your relationship. When I say extreme, I'm not alluding to violence or force. I'm saying that you need to get creative and do whatever it takes to have this conversation. If you just go to someone and say, "I've been thinking about cheating on you," they will respond defensively. You want to try to save face here. You want to use the words that truly express how you feel, but it's more important to express that something is missing. When key components of relationships go missing, this is when people cheat.

Someone will say, "Well, if they want to cheat, they should just leave." It's never that simple. If there are kids in the picture, leases, and lots of time invested, the easier thing to do is to cheat and hope the relationship will eventually get better. This is what most people do, and they do this because they lack the skills to work through the problems. People don't cheat because they don't want their partners. They cheat because something is missing. *If* they didn't want their lovers, then and only then would they break up. This is purely logical. Stop saying, "If you don't want to be with them, don't cheat—just break up." It's rational based on your value system, but to a person who is cheating, it doesn't make sense. Remember, we are trying to gain perspective from every single angle. It's not about trying to agree or disagree. Who cares what we agree with? We are here to explore all perspectives to increase our awareness. The more perspective we have, the more efficient we will be in our relationships. Stop passing judgment on people who cheat. A lot of them want help. Most writers, gurus, and media just blame them for their indiscretions and never give them the tools to succeed, like we're exploring here. Be less judgmental and more accepting of others. None of us are perfect. I'm a relationship mastermind, but I still make mistakes too.

If you're cheating, it's very important that you try to stop cheating as quickly as possible, because if you're good, it'll become addicting. You indeed do not want to play the addiction game, because then you start building another life outside of your relationship. Stop it immediately. Commit to the person you claim you're committed to already, and end the other nonsense right now. Just end it right now after reading this line.

4. Ask Yourself How You Would Feel

This is the easiest way to stop cheating. If you have a conscious and are a rational-thinking adult, simply ask yourself this question over and over. Take it one step further. I want you to truly visualize that person you claim you love, in the bed with another person. It will bother you to the nth degree to think about your partner in this manner. Consider this every single time you think about cheating. This will keep you at home and out of message threads that you have no business dealing with.

In closing, The relationship does not need to be online to be real. There's a lot of value in keeping this aspect of your life private. Your love life is special, sacred, and is a concoction of emotions, experience, and feelings. Share these moments with another soul, a soul that beats like the hearts in our little bodies. Nobody needs to know about your triumphs or failures. Everyone on this planet is love, but your love is sacred. Cherish what you have while you have it, and guard it at all costs.

Efficient Communication: The Second Pillar of Efficient Relationship Building

Background in Communication

I get the privilege, because of my career, to talk to so many different humans. The people I meet, through my art, open up and tell me everything they've been holding back. In fact, my natural personality is to listen, observe, and to give objective responses that stimulate thought and purpose. I remember doing this in high school, and since I am from an older generation, I remember sitting on the house phone and talking for hours with my girlfriend and other female friends. Honestly, it wasn't me doing the talking, actually. It was really a ton of listening and understanding. My environment gave me the opportunity to practice this skill, a skill that is necessary to master and practice for efficient relationships. I remember being so annoyed as a child, because my mom is a talker; she can be very deep, detailed, and passionate when she wants to be.

I remember sitting in the car and at grocery stores, feeling like a prisoner because she would strike up these conversations with strangers, and they would dive into the abysses of each other's thoughts.

I recall bugging and begging her to leave. "Ma, let's go. I'm ready to go home. It's hot out here." Mind you, if you've never experienced a Chicago summer, then you don't understand the special kind of hell that it feels like.

Humidity was my enemy as a child, and for whatever reason, my mother liked to compromise my comfort level. When she handed me ice cream and water, I shut up and didn't complain. In fact, I had timed when the ice cream truck would come around in my neighborhood, and she was so annoyed with me because I begged for that dollar. Since we're on the subject, I also ate the ice cream sandwiches, and there was another style called Choco Taco. She never gave me enough for both, but I could get two ice cream sandwiches for the dollar or wait a few days and get the Choco Taco for $2.50. Come on, people. I was kid, but I've always been smart. I understood the concept of saving money up very quickly. Plus, she wouldn't give me $2.50 for the Choco Taco. I'm not sure why. Maybe we were broke, or maybe she didn't want me to consume so much sugar, but I was the kid who played outside for eight hours at a time. In my kid brain, I needed the sugar in order to have energy. Which isn't true. You need fruits and vegetables, but that's another book.

My mother would get on the house phone and talk to people for six and seven hours at a time. Personally, I didn't have that much to say to anyone at all. I used to sit there, eating ice cream on those humid midwestern days, and think about who she was talking to. I would just sit in listen, like a student. I became a master communicator by observing and listening to my mother. She was the most dynamic person I ever observed around this idea of effective and ineffective communication. Like I explained in the last chapter, the goal isn't to grade anything as good or bad. That's too subjective and illogical actually. We are here to explore concepts on efficiency alone.

As a kid, I took notes in my journal, which I stole from the convenience store in my neighborhood. I hid this notebook between my bed frame and mattress, but I wrote in it every day. People always ask me, "How did you start writing?" This is the how and the why. My dad was always gone working, and my mom was talking to everyone and everybody, all of the time, no matter what. So I had to find a lane. My lane became writing because nobody was there to listen to me the way I wanted to be listened to. So I just had full-on conversations with myself, in my notebooks. My original notebooks contained my observations, as a kid, on human psychology. I broke down my observations of the relationship between my mother and father, as well as the ways they communicated with me.

Not to toot my own horn, but the only reason I do this professionally now is because I've literally done this my entire life. My writing style, somehow, grabs the user and brings you into my world, regardless of what doors you've previously closed. My writing style opens up everything, and it is because everything is relatable and based on human psychology. As I moved away from my youth, I only had interest in classes that explained human behavior—history, psychology, and communication.

I can't speak for anyone else, but the public school system education that I received was terrible—underpaid teachers who didn't want to be there, racism, bullying, and adults who hated their lives—yet I was forced to spend six hours per day with them, to ride the bus with psychotic children, and to endure curriculum that wasn't challenging or engaging. The cherry on top was that I was a gifted student and was forced to be in "school." I literally taught myself life skills, like ironing, cooking, and how to write poetry. My parents are owed a great deal of thanks because they had a good foundation for learning in the household. I owned by own thesaurus and dictionary and had the full set of the *Encyclopedia Britannica*. I didn't care about watching TV unless it was football or Nickelodeon. The reason I loved watching that station was because of the writing behind the shows. I was fascinated that there were people who could write stories. As a kid, I read the Goosebumps books over and over and over, mainly because the books were gripping and I wanted to learn how to get humans to listen to me, as a person, because they wouldn't. As my passion for writing grew, I started to understand human interactions. Like I said, my favorite classes were history, psychology, and communication. The latter two weren't even options until college, so I was only entertained in history, which gave me the best chance to master, understand, and introspect human behavior.

As a child, I annoyed my parents because I studied them for so long. Like a mad scientist, I knew how to manipulate them. The word *manipulate* has negative connotations, but since you're reading this objectively, you're not judging. In fact, manipulation is a common part of understanding power and motivation, which is directly connected to human desire. All of this is normal, my friends, but what I want you to understand is the person who understands how to manipulate any system, person, or group has the power. With great power comes the ability to impact and influence people in a positive way. You also have the chance to ruin good people and destroy lives, but don't be a stranger to understanding power simply because someone tells you to be meek and weak. You're reading Sylvester's work, so that means you already care about power and understanding humans. Since you're reading my words, it already means that you want to be and/or are already the highest version of yourself.

So let me connect the dots on how history, my mother, and all of my childhood stuff taught me how to be an effective listener.

There are many books, classes, and models that exist around communication, but I'm going to share with you what I have deemed as efficient based on my personal education and experiences. Again, I live pretty stress-free and have inner peace that really cannot be broken anymore. If you want to get to that point, take the notes you need and add what you want from my mind-set.

It was fifth grade, and I was at Holmes Junior High School in Arlington Heights, Illinois. I hated school with a passion, and I started to rebel. I had a cooking class, but since I was already teaching myself at home, I felt like I was above the classes, and I just made whatever I wanted. I had history right after cooking. One day in cooking class, we had to make some baked egg whites. I thought this was a terrible idea and a waste of the egg. They wanted us to crack the egg, separate the egg, bake the white, season it, and eat it like that. I found this to be disturbing and a waste. Instead, I used some available veggies and made an omelet for my group. My teacher tasted it and tried not to smile, but she still gave me an F since I didn't listen to her instructions. For me, this was the first opportunity I had in school to do what I wanted. The next hour I had history, and this was when it went down. This is the story of how I saw the power of listening. I'm painting this vivid picture because you have to put yourself in my shoes, at that time, in that place, for it to make sense.

Here I was, this young black kid in a school that was mixed, but when it came to history, black history was separated and marginalized. Of course, it was February, and that was when we talked about Black History Month. If any of you teachers have a gifted kid in your class, think of me. They are what I was in class. The teacher was a nice, sweet lady named Mrs. Lavender. I'll never forget this because her classroom was in the middle of the school, right across from the gym, and the cooking class was right next door, down the hall. I always sat by the door or window in my classes—in case a fight broke out, I could leave. The other benefit was because school was so boring, looking out the window or door gave me freedom as I created stories about the people who would walk by.

I'd tune back in to class and hear my teacher, the white lady, teaching me black history, and then I dropped a bomb.

Sylvester raised his hand.

The teacher looked at him and prepared herself for this unusual occurrence, because Sylvester never raised his hand or spoke unless he was called upon.

She called on him.

He said, "If I am American, and I am also black, isn't black history American history? If that is the case, we shouldn't have a separate month that marginalizes and forces us to learn about history during this month. Also, if this is about black people, why do I have to learn about it from white people? Are there not enough black historians around that can give us all a detailed and realistic account of what happened?"

She paused.

The room got silent and still, like a manmade lake.

My girlfriend, a Mexican girl named Wendy, just looked at me and didn't say a word, but I could feel her smile as she stared through me.

This was fifth grade.

Mrs. Lavender went on to tell me something I'd never forget. She said, "Sylvester, if I could go back to the 1960s, I would've been a freedom fighter, but I was too young. I would've been on the front line fighting for equality and happiness for all races. It's important to me to teach this section because I agree with you. Black people still have to deal with negativity, hate, and nonsense in this culture. I believe that teaching this helps give identity to my black students."

Then a silence cleared the air, and it was at that moment I understood the importance of listening.

Let's take a different look at this story.

Objectively, you have the young boy who was frustrated, confused, and entitled to his opinion. He actually attacked the teacher personally in his words, maybe not intentionally, but she had the chance to become upset. Especially when he mentioned he shouldn't have to learn this subject from a person of her race. She could've been hurt by this and punished him, scolded him, or made a fool of him, because of her position or paycheck. But no, she had the most efficient listening style any human could have. She listened not with her heart (subjective biases). She listened objectively to the facts and at no point took offense to the content.

Objective Listening

Objective listening is the ability to absorb all of the facts, stories, and moods of conversation without judging and grading them, regardless of your own personal bias.

We have to explore this together. What is the benefit of objective listening? Well, the last story, from all angles, was extremely sensitive, especially if you live in America—you understand how ignorant we are on the topic of race. Race is still a big deal in America. Racism is silly, if you ask me, but our country was made on division. We've divided ourselves up into social class, race, and every other type of separation. No human is born racist. It's impossible. That type of hate is taught and learned. Hopefully, the people who hate others because of their skin color will literally go away and be quiet.

Now, remember that this section is about how to effectively communicate. I'd like to explore what was said, plus her response, and let you come to your own conclusions about what happened next.

Be mindful of the age gap: a genius fifth grader and a teacher who was early thirties. They were able, in front of the pressure of other humans, to communicate in a deep way with intense and sacred emotions without actually hurting each other and adding to the conflict. What the student expressed was a boiled-up plate of conflict. The teacher didn't take it personally, and she only addressed the conflict, based on the information she had, with the consciousness level that she had.

She aligned.

Alignment—In every relationship there is a balance necessary, especially when it comes to listening. You don't need the right words all the time; in most cases you just need to align with people so they know they are understood.

All the teacher did was listen, repeat back, and paraphrase what was said to her, but with her story and viewpoint. This is what most of us need to do in our relationships. Most of us just react and overreact, and that path will always lead to an inefficient and lonely path. Don't seek to be right. Honestly, who cares if you're right? What benefit do you gain by being right? Does it benefit you if you prove that you're right and if your partner feels underneath you because of it?

I challenge you to expand your consciousness to a new level because two people can both be right, at the same time, even though their thought processes are opposite and conflictive. This only occurs once the people have confidence and inner peace in their messages. That fifth grader had valid and understandable claims, but so did she. They both spoke their piece, listened, aligned, and objectively responded to each other. Learning this skill right here can prevent *all* arguments in relationships. Literally, the arguing will cease to exist immediately if both people learn to shut up and listen objectivity. If you don't use objective listening now, that is okay, but I dare you to explore this with your partner. Do not expect anyone to get it right away. It may take years to learn this, and it's possible that you've been so conditioned to feel like you need to be right that you may never evolve to this, and that is okay too. Since you've seen this information and heard this story, you know that it is possible.

Yes, Mrs. Lavender became my favorite teacher because of this incident, and history stayed me favorite subject because of her. This objective-listening idea can make strides for your relationship right now. Being in a relationship is about listening. Listening is a skill, and on I'm going to give you three tips that I use all the time that will make your conversations more meaningful, empower your lover, and make you a better friend.

In this modern landscape it's not easy to get a generalization for the vibe. It feels selfish, self-centered, and ego based. It doesn't feel like community, like sharing and partnerships. I was listening to Dr. Umar Johnson speak on YouTube, and he has this thought, which I would like to expand. He believes that as a person you are either *individualistic* or you're a *nationalist*. The individualistic mind-set is when your focus is on your own agenda with a complete disregard for the bigger picture of the world, country, or family. This mind-set is fair to have because you're truly not responsible for anyone other than yourself, right? Well, the nationalist mind-set is one where your focus is the greater good for everyone. You believe in ideas like carpooling, bartering, and sharing. You want equal rights for everyone. A nationalistic person will sacrifice his or her own gain as long as it benefits the greater good of the company, nation, or peer group. It's my belief that if more people took the time to care and to be concerned with others, the landscape of this entire world would change. We need more empathy and more compassion as people. We can't sit here and blame society, because we are society.

It's your job and duty as a human to become a being of love; it's your job to listen to yourself, your spirit, your intuition. It is in divine order already. Stop listening to everyone else and align yourself with yourself. Listen to yourself. Once you practice listening to yourself, listening to others becomes extremely easy. If you want to be the best lover, friend, and person you can be, focus on your ability to listen. Listening is one of those intangible skills that cannot be measured, but it's imperative that you focus on it. The listening skill is by far one of the biggest skills missing, and it's mostly because people are individualistic. Most are looking out for themselves, which causes them to talk and not listen. Think of the community; be love; listen.

Stay Off Your Phone in Moments of Bondage—Engage

I'm about two seconds from walking over to this lady and taking her cell phone out of her damn hand. I am at a restaurant in Scottsdale, Arizona. I come here every time I am close to finishing my book-writing process. In fact, I travel to two places: San Diego and Sedona. Those places give me direction, peace, and clarity while I am close to finishing, and then I come to this little organic restaurant.

Now, I have on my red Beats by Dr. Dre headphones, and I'm listening to Yelawolf as the wind gusts across my face. It's a cooler day here in Arizona, and the mood is somber—yet perfect for me to grab you for this oh-so-important section of our *Dear Love Life*.

The lady is sitting across from a man. I don't see any rings on their fingers, but their behavior shows me that they have been together for a while. They seem very comfortable with each other; he is eating a sandwich, and she is devouring a salad.

They're sitting directly across from each other, but they're not exchanging energy or conversation. She's swiping through her phone, and he is looking around for engagement. Hold on—let me fake go to the bathroom so I can see what she is doing on her phone.

Wow, she's stuck in scroll abyss. It looks like a news site, but it doesn't look like anything important like checking the bank account to see who is paying for this meal. Objectively, I can see why this guy would seek companionship outside of the relationship. I can see why he would leave this relationship because, at least for this moment, there is no relationship.

Yes, couples have different rules and expectations for their relationships. Sometimes both people will eat while distracted and not speak to each other. I will never sit here and demand that you stay off your phone, because it's your life. In my mind and in my relationships, if we go out, what is the point of being on our phones? If we go out for drinks, food, or entertainment, there is no legit reason that a person has for being on the phone. If you have kids and they aren't with you, then I see a valid point. Let's not get too carried away with coming up with excuses to be disengaged in conversation.

Honestly, the expectation that there needs to be conversation at lunch is not what I'm pushing. I am saying that if two people who are developing a relationship wish to keep it going, they must take time to engage in conversations. I know how busy people can be now, and a lot of relationships only slow down once food gets involved. A lot of people are so focused on being so busy with school, work, and celebrities that they forget to be involved in their relationships. Honestly, I don't give a fuck what these celebrities are doing. If our relationship is suffering, we may both need to use a day of paid time off. Relationships are that serious to me. It blows my mind how people don't actually work on communicating and then wonder why their relationships suck. Later on, if this guy cheats or breaks up with her, she is going to act like she didn't see it coming, and then she will complain to her friends about everything she did do and how it still wasn't enough. Yet this man was basically begging her to pay attention to him. Friends and family, I'm here to tell you that everyone wants attention—men, women, and children. We all deserve to get attention from the person who claims to love us. This lady won't tell her friends how she neglected him, wasted his time, and was more concerned with the bullshit on her phone instead of the human being who was directly in front of her.

I'm literally amazed as I'm watching, because it just gets better. A random stranger just comes to their table, and I think it's a girl who works here. Hold on—let me fake like my headphones died and pretend to stretch so I can eavesdrop.

Okay, so check this out. This woman is fully engaged in a conversation with this stranger. Her man cleans the table, throws out the garbage, and stands there drinking his tea. His woman and this stranger are fully engaged in a conversation about ginger, the Jewish community, and living off of your kids. I couldn't make this up if I tried, people. This lady at no point introduces her man to this stranger, so he is standing there like an idiot, just watching. (This is an entirely different situation, but don't make your lover look stupid. If this situation happens to you, make sure you introduce your partner. It's only fair and shows respect.) Personally, I would've walked away while she talked, or introduced myself. There's no way that I would've just stood there like an idiot. Not that I would've been mad or angry, but clearly she showed she didn't need me in that conversation, so I would've moved on. That's just me.

This is valuable information for this dynamic because it shows me that this person really does not appreciate her lover. I want us to introspect and ask ourselves if we are this type of lover. Do we ignore requests for conversation and attention? We have to explore our behaviors around conversational connection and the expectations we have for each other. In some cases, I don't want to speak at all when I eat, and other times I want to hear all about her day. In order for us to have the most amount of power and efficiency in our relationships, it is crucial that we reevaluate our mentality about staying off of our phones while eating.

I believe this ideology can single handedly change relationships across the world because it allows us to organically connect to each other. In my relationship situations, I believe my partner has the right to do what she wants, so I will never demand, in that moment, that she stay off of her phone. I wouldn't recommend that you do it either, because demanding anyone to do anything doesn't sound efficient. I have two solutions for you. First, bring this concept up early and often, and if it's important to you, let your lover know that this is how you operate in that situation. Let her (or him) know your viewpoint on cell phones at the dinner table and while you're out to eat. Don't do it with the intent to control her, because again, she can do what she wants. Your goal should be to raise awareness. Some people don't see this as an actual problem, and I do. I think it's a huge problem. The second step you have to take involves you being the example, not just once but forever. You have to stay off of your phone—leave it off or in the car. You have to be the person to show her that you're serious about this behavior, because you do it. If you go out to eat and your phone is on the table, you're telling her, with your action, that this behavior is acceptable.

The cell phone phenomenon is actually causing a wide array of issues. Children do not need cell phones. A cell phone is a very powerful tool, and only users who know the full power should use it. I believe that to efficiently use a cell phone, you need a lot of control and discipline. Most users don't realize the psychological effects of using a cell phone. We get addicted to notifications because they release dopamine inside of us. These notifications help us feel loved and accepted. Even worse, social media actually allows us to get validation on our outfits or lifestyle changes. I believe this is one of the key causes to all problems in this generation. Instead of that lady getting the validation she needed from the man who was directly in front of her, she reverted to a device and the illusions that came across the screen. My friends, let's take control back and stay off of the phones as much as we are on them. It's more important to connect in real life, always.

The Top Three Listening Skills That Will Change Your Life ASAP

Paraphrasing

Do not be the annoying person who just simply repeats what was said to you and then says "huh." That person annoys me to the nth degree. I just think, "You heard what I said. Don't make me repeat myself." That's not what paraphrasing is. Paraphrasing is about summarizing what was said to you, in your own natural language, to send back into the universe. When someone is talking to you, he (or she) is the sender and you are the receiver. I can't stress enough how important it is for that person to understand that you heard what he said to you. Paraphrasing sounds like this: "I love how you said you would like to try kale because of its benefits. Do you have any idea what type of dish I could make you first?"

In this example, the receiver is telling the sender that he is thrilled about a new change, and the receiver even offers a solution to this person's change. It wasn't a closed-ended solution either. It was open, so it allows the person to continue the conversation, with vulnerability. Add paraphrasing to your package, and your relationship will improve.

Reassurance and Support

This has to be genuine and real in order for it to work, but it's a way for you to put the speaker at ease. All you have to do is help her through what she's talking about, if she struggles. If someone is opening up about a traumatic story or sharing a victory or even just something silly she's unsure of, you can change her comfort level. Many times, people are pressured to stop speaking, or they're not allowed to speak. What you have to do is listen to not only what they're saying, but you need to become intuitive enough to listen to each person's body language, pitch, and tone. An example of that sounds like this: "Listen to me. I am not judging you at all. I am a safe place to share that with. I will not judge you or put you down. Please share it with me." Or, "There is no pressure, but if you want to share, I am the ear that you need, now or forever."

If you say this to someone who is struggling, I'm willing to bet my next slice of pizza that you will empower that individual to open up the floodgates of vulnerability.

If this is new to you, practice with yourself. Write down a few things that you struggle with speaking about aloud. Read them to yourself in a mirror, put the notebook down, and then respond in a manner that you think another person would want to hear. Again, be genuine, and listen to your tone.

Stay Off Your Phone, Tablet, or Television

This may seem like a common-sense thing, but it isn't common sense. If it was, then people wouldn't focus on their phones, tablets, and TVs as much as they do and instead they would focus on human connection. But, sadly, people do it all the time. You and I have probably done it too, so we aren't going to sit here and blame anyone, as if we are the victims. No, we have all done this. I call this distraction or deflection. Some people refuse to accept this, and that is their own fault, because they suffer without even being aware of it.

Think of any device as a physical, emotional, and communicative barrier to success. If you're in a relationship, it will be considered a success once both parties feels like it is efficient, correct? When you pay undue attention to devices, you're literally communicating to a person, nonverbally, that their conversation, presence, or mood is not important to you. When I was a sales manager at Verizon Wireless, I demanded that my reps come from behind the cash register and greet the customers like human beings. There is no reason at all to wait for a customer to come over to you so you can slouch and lay around like a bum and say, "What can I help you with?" Hell no, we don't do that lazy stuff in my presence. You're required engage the customer in conversation. I apply this to my relationship. It's the only thing that I expect from the person I date. You and I will listen to each other. We will not be on the phone. We will engage and grow from the conversation, and there will be no barriers like cell phones. Focus on the people, not the device —that just supplies fake connections.

Understand the Concept

I get contacted by hundreds of people every single day looking for solutions and resolutions for their relationship situations. If people would understand this concept—stay off technological devices—a lot of pain would be alleviated.

But first, I want you to define the truth in your head. We often try to find the truth, but we look in places that don't seem trustworthy for the definition. Trust should come from internal introspection and awareness. Stop reading for a second, sit in silence, and ask yourself to define truth, right now. Yes, now. Stop reading. Pause. Take a moment to explore this topic. Your feelings are not a TRUE reflection of the entire situation. Your own personal biases do not equate to the truth. To find the truth one must always remain objective and observant.

> "To be effective in a relationship you have to accept that both of you can be true, even if the truth is opposite or different."
> - Sylvester McNutt III

What Is the Truth?

I turned to Snapchat one day to ask everyone to tell me what they thought the truth was. I received about four hundred messages back from people, in video format, explaining to me what they felt like the truth was. The ironic part about my position in that moment was how I was able to listen to, literally, four hundred definitions of the same thing, and they were all different.

Yes, I have my own definition of the truth, and then I realized a key point. The truth is always subjective, and therefore it's not logically based on what everyone feels like is a fact. The truth is always subjective based on the individual's bias, level of awareness, and perception of the world; that doesn't make it right or wrong.

When I first had this thought, I immediately rejected it, because I think like you, and I thought of some real-world analysis like "The earth is round, and that is a fact, and so if a person says it's round, it's the truth." Then I thought objectively again and realized that it's not true, because there are people who died thinking the earth was flat. Books and teachings existed around this premise that the earth was flat. Don't judge this; observe it. Realizing this made me understand that people can at most do the best they can with what they have, based on who they're are and what they have experienced.

Yes, people can only communicate and understand from the levels of consciousness that they're currently operating at. So every person is experiencing his or her own first-person narrative. Remember that none of us can see the end of our own movies. We are all watching our plots, hearing the themes, and feeling the conflicts of our own movies.

I'm commanding you to look at things in the third person, especially your own self, because you hold all of the power to change, grow, and improve. If a person is hell bent on proving to me that her truth is based around the earth being round, do you know what I have to do if I want to be happy, healthy, and in a state of peace around this person?

Yes, you guessed it. I have to accept this person, as she is today, because my truth cannot and does not negate hers, regardless of how factual I may believe my truth to be. This concept is life changing and monumental from the aspect of getting along and communicating inside of a relationship.

It's okay, normal, and acceptable to have two opposing thoughts or ideas. You don't have to be right, prove your truth, or fight another person's viewpoint.

Especially if this is a person whom you're trying to be around often. Why would either one of you continue to bicker, not see eye to eye, and resent each other because of very small misunderstandings. Ladies and gentleman, it is perfectly okay not to disagree or agree. There is nothing wrong with just listening without judging or having an opinion. If we spent more time just being interested instead of being upset and mad, our entire relationship structures would change. Listen and align.

No matter what you do or how you maneuver, you can't argue with this, because I live this every day. I accept that my truth and another's truth do not have to negate each other. Once you accept that the other person is allowed to have whatever concept she wants, then and only then will you tap into inner peace inside of a relationship.

Internal Value Systems and Ratings: Internal Communication

I'm sitting here on my Xbox One, playing this game called Mortal Kombat X, and I am thinking about the characters that I pick while I battle to the death—in virtual reality of course, not in real life. If for some reason you are a person who has never heard of Mortal Kombat, allow me to introduce you. This is the most successful fighting game of all time. People have been fighting in Mortal Kombat on video game consoles across the world since it was established in 1992. I'll be right back to go play a few rounds since you don't know about Mortal Kombat. Go Google it, you caveman.

I'm back. I lost my first match to some kid who kept squealing. He gave me an instant headache, so I got off because I couldn't deal with his prepuberty voice, so I'm back to my job, which is sharing stories and perspectives. (Did you Google it yet?)

But why did I lose? Yes, I'm going to use a video game analogy to describe something in your love life, and then you're going to use it with your kids for brownie points. We call that the circle of life.

I played with a character called Scorpion, and I fought a character named Sub-Zero. Scorpion is a fast ninja that does not have a lot of special moves, but if the user is quick, he can be the most confusing person to fight since he teleports and can shift his angle of attack. Sub-Zero has the ability to freeze you and throw ice at the character he is fighting, and he can protect himself from projectiles with an ice shield that he summons upon command.

In sports, these character traits are referred to as ratings or attributes. Friends, think about this logically. If I pick up a video game controller to the play the game, obviously I want to win, so I am going to pick the players, fighters, and team that give me the best chance of winning, right?

If you play a basketball video game, then you are aware that the ratings are based on the players' real-life performances, right? Then you should pick the Warriors or the Cavaliers. Why? Because LeBron James and Steph Curry are the best players in basketball; the Warriors are the highest-ranked team. Odds are, you'll win more games with those two teams versus any other, right? This is basic logic. In my opinion of Mortal Kombat, Tanya is the best character. She is the fastest, has moves in the air and ground, and can teleport. I can fight anyone with this skill set. I would be confident in fighting anyone with Tanya, right now, regardless of how good a person might be. I have the utmost confidence and respect in Tanya.

Guys, please read this objectively. No matter what truth we want to believe, we have our own ratings, and we rate other people based on their attributes, values, and abilities. As much as we refuse to openly acknowledge it, I'm just giving you the truth and being realistic. If we were to be created in a video game, what qualities would you bring to the table? If someone picked you to fight for his life, what would be his hardest struggle with dealing with you as his character?

This is about self-awareness and self-awareness only. Seven out of eight people do not know what they bring to the table other than some recycled garbage that they've heard on the Internet. Again, I don't want you to judge yourself from a moral standpoint. Don't be subjective and emotional in said judgment; simply observe yourself as you are, and you will find the answers.

If you date Sylvester, you will get a man who will believe in you and will motivate you to be the best woman you can be, and a man who will try his best to have fun and laugh with and at you. Sylvester's biggest struggle is his art. His art attracts the attention of a lot of women. His art requires a massive amount of his time, and it's not a normal job, so there are not set hours for when he works.

See, it's not about judging yourself as good or bad. It's just about becoming aware of who you are.

Yes, being a writer is an amazing thing, but it attracts a lot of women. Now, this could be detrimental and inefficient when I try to date, but since I'm aware of it, I can win. I know that I have to date a woman who is secure in who she is. I don't want to waste time defending my work, which would happen if I date an insecure woman. At the same time, I know that I have to make sure I'm transparent and honest so she can thrive inside of my environment. Also, since I believe that humor is a big factor in the relationship, I won't waste a lot of time with someone who doesn't want to laugh or a person who is always mad. It's very possible that I will like and care for someone like that, which is normal. But it's even more probable that some people just don't line up from a value-system standpoint.

This to me is one of the deadliest things I see people do in relationships now. They invest a little bit of time and just stick around, regardless of how toxic two people are for each other. This is something that I will never understand, ever, but people are allowed to do what they wish. I notice that people will stick around and try to control their lovers, or they wish their partners would be something they're incapable of being. This is so dangerous. Look—everyone has different value systems, and if they don't align, regardless of how much you care, it just won't work, and that is real. I do not believe that value systems, ratings, and attributes have to align with every single thing. Two mature, logical, and open-minded adults have the ability to accept each other's differences. Some of you suffer because you're trying to fit a square box into a round hat, and that will never happen, ever. It's impossible. I guess the real question is this:

> How long can you survive trying to force compatibility? How long will you survive in situations where you feel like you have to change people in order to love them? These are the real questions, because that mind-set is about force and control, and that is not love. If you love them, let them breathe. If you can't accept them, they might not be the problem—it might be you.

Understanding value systems and ratings directly correlates with what I said earlier about "listening to yourself." This is what I call *internal conversation*. In a lot of cases, people sit and wait for others to see their worth. They bank on hopes and dreams, and they get so far away from reality. Personally, I'll never promote breakups and pettiness. However, I do believe that some people do not match. Some people can't be together no matter how much they think they care about each other. I will promote that suffering isn't necessary. Suffering is a choice. One of the oldest clichés of life fits so well right here: If you took a square peg and tried to fit it into a round hole, what would happen? This is truly about becoming in tune with yourself, understanding that you can never control or change anyone, and finally accepting that you might not truly fit into a person's value system. I don't want you to suffer, and if you're not a fit, you just can't force it. You'll save yourself years and years of time by not trying to force compatibility and peace with someone. There's a major difference between two people who have problems and just need help and two people who don't match. We all have problems, and that's one situation that can be improved. But when you just don't match, you can't prove yourself to this person. You truly have to let it go or suffer—it's your choice.

Commitment Is Efficient Communication

To commit is an action. We must understand that commitment is always about actions and nothing more. An action is something that is completed via the observation of one's behaviors. It requires physical proof. It does not matter what I say, if my actions do not align, there will be confusion. The confusion will come because my actions do not align with the ideology I am claiming that I want. This is called *cognitive dissonance* in psychology. In life, things don't align, and the reason they don't align falls into two categories: our actions or our perceptions.

Nothing of value occurs without commitment, period. If you want to get a six-pack, you have to commit to eating well and exercise. If you want to write a book, you need a subject and to write every day. If you want to put $10,000 in your bank account right now, you need to increase you income while reducing your expenses. These are different concepts, but they require the same idea: commitment.

It behooves me to see how many people do not commit to actually being in a relationship. Plus, it floors me to see how people wonder why their towers of love are crumbling to the ground. If there is no commitment, then there is no relationship. The commitment is the foundation. All structures need a base to stand on—why don't people get that? Here is the deal. I would never preach that anyone should chase a particular title; in fact, I believe that my teachings are going to teach something that hasn't been talked about in modern dating. Can we be honest with each other? I've seen married people take their rings off and have sex with people who they aren't legally committed to. I've seen the most disrespectful, disloyal, and selfish humans do things, in regard to dating, that proves they don't deserve others' love.

But these people move in the darkness. They move in the shadows, posing as positors of love even though they are just mongers of hate here to drag you through an emotional war that will have you fighting yourself daily. Honestly, we don't know who those people are, and they might even be you and I.

Of course people can change, but that doesn't change the damage that has been done. You've experienced trauma, loss, and heartbreak before, and I don't want you to do it again. This book is preparation for that, but what I'm about to tell you is something others won't say, because they are scared and aren't realistic. After I say this, you can decide what you really believe, in but I *dare* you to double think this over after reading the entire book.

> Don't chase titles at all. They don't mean anything without consistent action backing them. Titles are just ways other people can define what you're doing, and they don't promise happiness, longevity, or anything of value.

Here's the deal. I grew up in America, and in America we are run by the media. News outlets, the Internet, and social media control us. Our movies, music, and entertainment activities are basically the most important thing to us here in America. I cannot speak for other countries, because I wasn't raised there, but I can say that most people, especially women, have their love life given to them based on media.

American women are conditioned to see that it's okay to be a damsel in distress because a man will save them. It's okay and normal to spend lots of money on a party (wedding) because it's all about the ceremony. And there's a timetable for when and how all of this stuff will occur.

It's possible that men have these fairy tales in their head about how their love lives will go, but I've never met a man who tried to predict that stuff. Sure, you're allowed to desire whatever you want, but wishing for someth happen more than experiencing it is emoti suicide if it doesn't happen.

Yes, some women are given this vision, and they manifest it. However, I'm here to tell you that the dating landscape has changed. It's a very competitive sport, in my eyes, and I feel like the most successful woman in today's world is going to be one who lives day to day and is mindful.

In my mind, a wedding shouldn't be a party at all. As men, if we meet women who only talk about this fantasy, their relationship goals, and everything they want in matters of love, it is typically a turnoff. It makes the guy think, "Damn, does she want me, or am I just a placebo for the fairy-tale idea that she has around love?"

Be present and reduce the expectations of the future. The future is an illusion because you really have no clue what will happen. You might lose your arm tomorrow. I'm not here to spread doubt or shade on marriage. I am not that person. I am only telling you to be the most powerful person you can be by being present, today, and you can do that without chasing titles. Titles cause stress, confusion, and in most cases, unrealistic expectations.

I'll never forget how deserving I felt to get promoted to indirect account manager when I was just an assistant manager. I wanted the more prestigious title, the one that had a bigger salary and came with more respect and power within the corporation.

This wanting and overthinking behavior created so much stress and anxiety, I lost complete appreciation for my current situation. I lost the ability to be happy in my current role, like I was before because I deemed I was ready and worthy for the next role.

At that time, you couldn't have convinced me that I wasn't ready, but that was not my path. I was never supposed to get that role, because it would've killed me. I wasn't happy, because my passion was writing, and I wasn't doing that full time. I wasn't as healthy as I could've been, and I had too many toxic people around me.

My friends, this could very well be you too. Don't hurt your brain obsessing about a title and lifestyle change. Truthfully, it's not about the titles that we search for—it's only about the feelings we create inside of our own selves and others.

Remember, titles are just place marks for conversations. Everything worth talking about lies in the actions of you, me, and every other human walking the planet. If I am in a car accident and I wake up to see that you are standing over me helping me when I can't help myself, I am not going to say, "Are you a brain surgeon?" Your behavior is showing that you are a loving, caring, and empathic person, and in that moment you are trying to save a life, regardless of title.

What if one of your titles was felon? That shouldn't change how much I value you in the situation. It's always about the present moment and present behaviors. It's about us showing what is inside over and over and over. If you're literally saving my life, how am I to judge you because you're a felon? That's ridiculous, and that is why I say to be present. Be mindful of the behaviors that you have, because they are the relationship, and most importantly, don't break your back or happiness chasing a title. The worst thing you can do is grade a situation based on the title. Just because you're a felon doesn't mean you're going to hurt me, and just because you're a doctor doesn't mean you're going to help me.

How Do You Obtain a Commitment from Dating?

I get this question a lot from people, and the only realistic answer is this: communicate openly from day one, communicate about each other's desires and goals, and be as honest as possible, because if your friendship is built on communication, the commitment behaviors of conversations will always be easy and appropriate.

If you meet someone, that person is not looking for a relationship commitment from you on day one—that is unrealistic.

In the very beginning, it should be about breaking the ice and finding out about each other's value systems. In the beginning it also should be about being present in each date and interaction so each moment can be genuine. Dating is a process of becoming friends and is sparked by interest, attraction, or desire.

That is my definition of dating. Most people do not understand what dating means. Dating does not make you sexually, emotionally, or physically exclusive to anyone. It only means that you're willing to get to know someone. This can be one person or multiple people at a time. If you're dating, you have to be honest in order to be efficient. Meaning if you're open to meeting and entertaining multiple people, that should be stated in a natural, organic way. People develop emotions, and that is normal. To disregard the feelings that develop just because you're unsure of how you feel is egregious and irresponsible. But to force a commitment ultimatum or conversation on someone when the situation may not warrant it, from both sides, is also just disrespectful. There is such a thing as being too clingy too fast, and that is subjective to each person's value system. It's very possible that we can meet day one and start our committed relationship right there. It's not probable, but it is possible. To be efficient, you have to communicate through these processes, and you have to understand that you might not get your desired outcome when you want it. That is okay and acceptable too.

Fear and Noncommitment Introspection
Yesterday I was afraid of commitment, and I didn't even understand why. I literally was sitting here asking myself, "Why haven't you committed to this woman who is amazing?" She has work to do. She has potential. She has red flags. But doesn't everyone? This is the internal conversation I had with myself, and I am only sharing with you because you may relate. You may gain power from my personal introspection. Please view objectively and take notes for your own self.

I can sit here and nitpick and wait for something better to come along, or I can take the really great person that is directly in front of me and commit to her.

I get it—trust me. I do. We are the generation of entitlement and confusion. We would rather dive into rounds of sex, alcohol, and drugs before we obtain a commitment. It's laughable actually, because we are all a bunch of broken adults running around stabbing each other like two people who enjoy pain. Ouch. Yes, the truth hurts, and it's not men or women. It's not black or white. It's not poor or rich. It's all of us. We are all killing each other in these love games, mostly because we refuse to commit. But think deeper than what you're thinking right now. You're thinking about a relationship commitment in terms of obtaining a title. You're first instinct is to think about this concept of obtaining the commitment of boyfriend/girlfriend and then husband/wife. I am here to remind you, tell you, or explain to you that without commitment, you are never going to obtain these phases of life that you claim you want, but even still, I need you to think much deeper. Each phase requires a commitment to certain behaviors, understanding, and environments. Let's use this chapter to face some fears, be objective, and establish a vibrational awareness around this concept.

Commitment and Risk

Do you ever sit and just ponder what a risk is? Have you ever really sat there, with an open mind, and just allowed your mind to float down the river of curiosity, especially around risk?

A risk is exposure to danger, harm, or loss. Of course, risk is normal. Risk and the concept of analyzing it have been around since the beginning of time. There are different risk styles that we all go through, based on personality types and the awareness of different situations. There was a time when a man could only survive if he hunted daily and took multiple risks to find food. Risk was literally a life-or-death matter. That has not changed. Ultimately, we have an abundant access to food and resources, but if we do not risk taking a chance, we risk a spiritual, emotional, and even a physical death.

Risk Averse—I found this term in an economics class I took in college. Basically, it refers to investors who do not like much risk as far as their returns are concerned. They would rather take the lower reward based on the fact that they only see the value in risking a little.

Risk Taker—This term is pretty self-explanatory. A risk taker will take a great risk without guarantee or promise that such move will garner a specific result.

Some people in this generation are afraid of commitment, but why? The concept of commitment doesn't only apply to relationships in the intimate sense. Commitment seems to be an ideal and moral that has become less fashionable these days. I want to instill a seed in your head that I believe will blossom into something great if you water it. People who fear commitment are normal-thinking people for this society. It makes sense to fear it because there appears to be a lot of valuable options that are easily accessible, and that is true. Don't look at it is a bad thing at all, but social media, dating sites, and just the overall mood have made it really easy to get sex, to get attention, or to attract someone to spend time with. I highly recommend you become, remain, and preach commitment to your friends and family. It's the ultimate prize, I believe, to build a friendship and relationship and then a family with another human being. There isn't a perfect human walking this planet, so no matter who, when, or where, it will require work and effort, and that is the beautiful part of this human amalgamation.

If you yourself have feared commitment, don't think of it as if that fear is a bad thing, and if you find people who are a little bit scared, don't force them into commitments. If people do not want to commit, that is their choice, and they're allowed that.

If they don't want to commit, do not kill your self-esteem and view of yourself. Remember that all humans have the right to choose what they want to do. If and when someone commits to you, cherish that person.

How to Get a Man to Commit to You

If he does not respect you, he won't commit or treat you as well as you think you should be treated. Men treat women in two ways: how they see you from their perspective and how you allow yourself to be treated. To get a man to truly feel the need to commit be his peace, add value to his life, and always respect yourself.
—Sylvester McNutt III, "Prize."

This next subject is my favorite of all time to talk about with women, because when I hit the bullet points, I see the light bulbs go off in their heads. I had a small-group talk last night, and this was the subject. I gave people the opportunity to chime in and took their feedback. This section will read as a summary of what we talked about.

They were asking me about why I like my girlfriend and what makes men commit to women just in general. I explained this concept to my girlfriend last night. I can't speak for all men, but this may explain some men.

Why Do I Like Her—I like her because I have a lot of respect for her. I like the way that she talks to me, and 98.75 percent of the time, I like the way she carries herself. Respect for men is fragile. I truly believe it is the most important component of mental attraction for men. See, our biology tells us to be attracted to all of the women that we like looking at, but that won't determine if a man will *want* to treat a woman well. No man is going to stop finding other women attractive. That's unrealistic. I laugh when I hear girls say things like, "I only want my guy to have eyes for me." It sounds great in the movies, but if we're talking about reality, your dad, every man you can possibly date, and even I will notice other attractive women. We have to be realistic. Yes, we are going to look at attractive women when their pictures pop up online; yes, we are going to notice them walk into restaurants; and yes, we may even have sexual fantasies about women that we have no emotional attachment to. This is a possibility of having the male biology.

As a woman, you can sit inside of suffering and think that you can control a man's thoughts, or you can realize that this stuff is normal and not a big deal. So many girls reach out to me and ask me if they should break up with their men based on the fact that they liked photos on Instagram. One, you should be more secure with yourself as a woman, and two, just because someone likes on a photo, that doesn't mean you should break up with him. This is such a ridiculous thought to me.

But is attraction the most important thing to a man? No, absolutely not. It's important, yes, but after that, what else is out there? But attraction alone isn't enough to make a man commit and treat a woman well. I talked to a few good married men about this, and they flat out said, "I respected my wife from the beginning. She would've never allowed me to do her the way I did the other women. I wanted to change for her, so I did." The other married man said, "She was just different than all of the other girls. She said that she wanted me to be the happiest man in the world." It is so important that a man feels respected, feels like he respects his woman, and feels like he lives in a dating environment where there is consistent respect.

I'm thinking of all of the recent toxic situations I've been hearing about related to the way a man treats his woman, and I can honestly say that it boils down to respect. My mind-set on respect is twofold. First, I believe that respect and the perception of respect is internal and based on that individual's value system. Second, I believe that any person you interact with, especially a loved one, has the ability to learn what respect is to you. If you really want to be with someone, I believe that it is imperative you learn about that person's views of respect and disrespect.

I don't really want to come online to see my woman bragging about a booty picture online. Is it disrespectful? I don't know, but I do know it's personally not something I want to deal with. For me, it's disrespectful when a woman yells at me or calls me names. It's disrespectful to threaten me, to give me ultimatums, or to spend your time emotionally cheating on me. This is specific to me. These are instant disrespect triggers for me personally, and if a woman does these things, it pushes me away. I only list these things as a blueprint for understanding, because all people are different. Learn your man. Don't be hardheaded and think that you know how to be with a man and that it is easy. Stop it. Learn your man day after day.

Value-System Awareness

This is literally the most important facts when it comes to getting a man to commit to you. When I refer to commitment here, I am referring to the whole ten yards: the title, the behaviors, consistent effort, sexual commitment, emotional commitment, as well as any other qualities that women look for when they want commitments from guys. What I'm observing through my shows, clients, and observations is that there are too many people trying to force connections. There's a certain balance that has to occur between people synching up and then molding together. I believe that nobody wants to be lonely, so we end up settling for situations, even if there is no sure commitment in them. Obviously, some people who have situationships are very happy. Some want more. This text is here to serve the purpose of giving more insight around possible ways to get more. Some people have no problem with this, but some do. I know this perspective will provide you a ton of mental freedom. I have two thoughts on the levels of this:

A. The Organic Connection

B. The Effort Connection

The Organic Connection

In some cases, two people can be so compatible that it is very easy for them to commit with little to no effort at all. I'll introspect myself, since I am a man, and give you a woman who would organically connect with me, day one. A woman who is into health, humor, and happiness. A woman who likes to have deep conversations, but at the same time she's all about having fun. I don't eat meat, so if she doesn't eat meat, there will be more of an alignment. My favorite hobbies are writing and yoga, so if she is into those, that would instantly make her more attractive to me. From a moral standpoint, I don't believe in violence in the relationship or with children. I also believe that the man and woman have separate roles in the relationship and that they need to respect each other's energy. In situations when I meet a woman like this, I instantly want to commit to her—literally instantly. She is the type of woman I will build with instantly, and the reason for that is that, as a man, all of those things are very important to me, so for her to rank very high on my value-system scale, commitment will come quicker rather than later in this scenario.

Here's where this gets fun. Most women are taught to introduce their representatives to men, so they're wasting dates. A lot of women are so scared to be judged and looked at in a negative light that they don't show their true colors from day one. They play it safe, and they're just nice. They go with the flow of the date. As a woman, on the first few dates your goal should be to find out about his value system, not to find out about his past. His past really is irrelevant, and so is yours. I strongly urge you to ask a man these three questions on dates. Doing so will impress him. It will be genuine for you, and it will give both of you an awareness to know where you're going to rank on his value system.

1. Tell me about your business plans, and if we work out in the future, what role do you think I would have in it?

This question is the most important question you can ask a man, in my opinion. It's multilayered and does a few things that actually give you the full advantage as a woman. The first thing it does is force him to think about a future with you, and that means commitment. That means that by even answering this question, you're giving him the option to think about committing to you, and if this is a solid guy, that is what you want. Remember that you're a stranger to him at this point, so he may say, "I don't have any plans with you yet. I just met you." If he says anything like that, don't worry, because that's fair. However, a man of ambition might actually have a plan or desired role he would want his woman to have in his life.

This question is one of the easiest ways to empower your man and to show him that you believe in him. I highly recommend doing this the very first day. Use your personality, and set it up after a few hours of talking. If the vibe is right, then it should come off natural and easy. Ask him in a fun and joking manner, and laugh. As much as I'd like to believe that men are leaders, I truly believe that a woman who understands psychology and controls her emotions is the most efficient and powerful human being. If you need to, practice-ask one of your guy friends this question. Obviously, the dynamic is different, so if you're not trying to date the guy friend, do not ask him with you inserted as the possible female figure. Ask him, "What role do you want your future woman to have in your life in regard to helping you build your business?"

The reason you ask this question is so you can observe your prospective lover's body language and response. Do not ask this question using text message. Obviously, if he has a job, business, or is in school, find out how you can contribute. If he is struggling and is unemployed, doesn't own a business, and isn't in school, do not ask, because it will emasculate him.

2. **What is your current dating situation, and more importantly, if you vibe with the right girl, where would you like to be?**

It amazes how many women never ask guys what they're doing. Don't ever ask a guy this over text message. Ask him in person, face to face, after you've talked with him. I honestly expect women to ask me this on the first date, and I would say that 5 percent of the women I've dated have asked this at all.

As a guy, I'm going out with you because I have a sexual attraction to you. I might not have any desire to be with you. I think you're attractive, and my male brain is telling me to create a sexually charged situation so I can have sex with you. That is why we go out on first dates. Yes, it's very possible that a man will be looking for more, but how does he know he wants more from you when he doesn't know his value system? I know this is hard for some women to understand, because some women like to get to know guys before they have sexual interactions. That is okay too, but what I want you to understand is that we want to have sex. It's not sad; it's biology. Knowing and accepting this gives you the power and advantage in dating. The women who do not accept this as law are the ones who end up hurt, heartbroken, and jaded because they have unrealistic expectations of men. Ladies, I'm giving you male psychology: he wants sex, period. He doesn't know you at the beginning or your value system, so the only guaranteed thing that you're worth is sex.

Asking him this question forces him to tell you if he is married, has a girlfriend, or if he is fresh out of a relationship. If you don't ask, you're leaving the burden on him to be honest, and it's not his fault if he doesn't tell you. Look—some men are unhappy in their relationships, and they seek excitement and fun outside of them while working on them. Look—I'm not justifying it. I'm just telling you what I have seen. If you are the type of woman who doesn't want to settle for that type of situation, you have to ask, from day one.

This lets him know a few things. For you, his answer to this question gives you insight to what he has been doing and what he thinks he is going to be doing. Do not just flat out ask if he has a girlfriend or wife. Highlight that last line, because if you ask that, you will set yourself up for failure. If he is separated, he isn't obligated to tell you that he is technically still married. If he isn't technically together with a woman, he isn't required to tell you that he is still sexually active with his ex. Do not ask the closed-ended question of "Do you have a girlfriend and/or wife?" You have to ask him the open-ended question that I listed above. An open-ended question forces the other person to talk in detail, even if it is just a sentence. Dating is about psychology and information, so it is your job to get the information by being prepared. After I give you the third question, you'll be more prepared than 99 percent of the women in the world.

3. **If you could sit down with any famous person and have a conversation with that person, what would you talk about and why?**

This is a great question to start off with, but it's also a very important question, and the reason why is because he will let you know more about his value system. This type of question allows him to be vulnerable, honest, and deep. As a woman, your job is to get him to open up, which is damn near impossible because most women in this generation do not have the tools to understand male psychology.

All of these questions can actually pad his ego and will not emasculate him. These questions give him the organic ability to open up, and they give you valuable information you may need to continue seeing this guy. Plus these questions are all fun, easy to remember, and do not create stress or pressure. They allow you to get deep, but they're worded in a way that is not intrusive. Using these and other questions formatted in this way will keep you high on his value system, now and forever. The main reason I want you to do this is because these will help you in the process of figuring out if you are an "organic connection" to him, based on his value system, and the answers to these question provide you with valuable information.

The Effort Connection

The effort connection is actually way tougher and is more of a realistic occurrence in this dating generation. In most cases, it's going to take a massive amount of communication, experience, and time with each other to get the woman to a level where the man sees her as valuable enough to commit to. There are many ways to create an organic connection, but if people do not pay attention to communicating openly, then it's literally impossible. In my experience and observation, most women want to play it safe, and they create the effort connections because they don't ask the open-ended questions. They're not open enough within the dates, and because they simply do not line up that much, it will take communication and effort—one just easier than the other.

There are some women who will flat out reject this concept, and that is okay too. This writing is not here to instill any type of insecurity in women. It's not here to force unnatural behavior. I've been a male my whole life and have had very candid conversations with other males about this topic. I just want to help, and I feel as if this information gives all women an advantage when dating, because knowledge and psychology are true power.

Nobody Can Read Minds Communicate Clear and Effective Messages

In relationships, we do not have time to play guessing games of how the other people feel. One of the hardest things for a person to do is invest and give everything to a person when she (or he) doesn't know where that person stands. It is imperative that you communicate effective messages by using your nonverbal body language, your technology, and your mouth. Communication will be the rise and fall of your dating situation.

We get it. Some people may consider themselves to be introverted. Some people may consider themselves to be shy. Some men may not feel like they can speak up, because society forces them to silence all emotions. Some women may feel everything so deeply that they don't know how to communicate what they feel. Some people don't feel anything at all. You are all entitled to be, feel, and think whatever you'd like about your own self. I am not going to tell you to get out of your own head. I won't tell you to stop overanalyzing. The raw and honest truth is this: A relationship is not solely about you. It requires that you grow and adjust so the other person can be happy too. Love requires that you step outside of your box.

Yes, that means you have to get uncomfortable so the other person can be comfortable. Your relationship should have a *nationalist* type of feel, not an *individualistic* type of feel. Do it for her; do it for him. Get off of your self-entitled, victim-focused mind-set that prohibits growth. Once you develop a consistent lane of communication, all of those insecurities and inefficient behaviors around communicating go away because of practice. You'll never be good at communicating if you don't practice. Stop putting your ability to communicate how you feel and think on others and their responses. That's not fair. That's an illogical approach to dating and communication. It is your goal to evolve, to become the greatest communicator that you can be. This will tip over into your career, your friendships, and your relationships. You really only have two options: communicate clearly and have peace of mind that you've put it all out on the table, or do not communicate effectively and allow confusion, conflict, and suffering to enter your relationships and yourself.

It is illogical to think that because a person has been with you a certain amount of time that he should just know how you feel or think. Yes, part of the evolution of relationships is the learning process. The process that allows you to know your partner's favorite foods, sleeping habits, and even the type of movies he'll (or she'll) pick on Netflix. It's an amazing love story when you guys start to share common interests and can finish each other's sentences. It really is the greatest poem ever written. However, expecting someone to "always get it" is illogical and will bring you guaranteed suffering. Over time, people's interests and desires change. Your skin sheds every month, your taste buds change every few months, and you grow out of certain tastes. Ten years ago all I listened to was hip-hop music. Now, I'm all over the board. As we age, we change. As we move, we grow. Don't ever assume that anyone should just "get you." People get you because you communicate who you are today, every day, not because of who you were. Are you the same person you were one year ago? No, so stop expecting anyone to "just get you." If you believe you should just be "gotten," you're agreeing to the idea that you don't change and that you have and will always be the same person. I guarantee that you don't believe that, because you're presently reading a self-help book. The body of the text here only exists to improve, to alter, and to change lives.

There's no way you're reading this book just to stay the same.

Say what you mean, and mean what you say. Make sure that you communicate how you truly feel and think, because others need to know who you are. You honestly might not be the best person to be around. Don't trap anyone into a web of lies and confusion because you have charm but can't communicate. Give everyone the free will they deserve by giving the information as it comes. Give them the real information. It's imperative that you focus on being this type of person, because the odds of you attracting a person like this increase greatly. It's so much easier to be in a relationship where both people feel like they can communicate openly, without fear or judgment. You create the most efficient type of relationship once you abolish the walls that society has placed on your relationship. You create longevity and substance once you allow your relationship to breathe, to be naked and raw like the jungles in Southern America.

Respect: The Third Pillar of Efficient Relationship Building

What would happen if you stood on the edge of a cliff, when the wind was blowing at fifty miles per hour? Odds are, since you didn't respect gravity, the sheer set up of the geographical difference in height and force of the wind would most likely push you over. What would happen if the video game Frogger, became real life? How confident would you be that you can jump between lane and lane, avoiding cars that are trying to hit you? These are tough situations because it appears that there's a lack of respect for the outcomes and possibilities of danger. Respect is a feeling of deep admiration for someone or something elicited by his or her abilities, qualities, or achievements. I believe that once you truly respect your partner, your morals, and you relationship ideologies, it is impossible to have an inefficient relationship. Respect combined with effective communication and trust is the blueprint for success for all effective relationships. I stand behind this thought and will take it to my grave that this is the most important pillar to focus on. When actions, conversation, and tones are built off of respect, everything has a chance to prosper. In fact, could you imagine trying to have a garden in soil that was polluted and full of acid? Your crops wouldn't grow that well. But what happens once you respect each other, nourish each other, and put your desires inside of soil that can handle it? The three pillars that I harp on are respect, communication, and trust, and what I want you to accept is that respect builds into the other pillars.

Chapter 4

Introspection, Self-Awareness, and Self-Understanding—the Missing Components in Modern-Day Relationships

One day I was sitting outside in nature, allowing the vibrations of the earth to send chills up and down my spine. I had something heavy on my mind and heart—an amount of pain that I couldn't understand or process. I couldn't figure out why I kept striking out when it came to dating and relationships.

Personally, my relationships were always pretty fun, but dating was never fun, mainly because it takes people forever to be their real selves, and I present that on the first day. Dating is the art of getting to know someone, which includes going out to establishments or just hanging out around each other. But being in a relationship means that both people have committed verbally and with their actions to build and grow the relationship. In my personal experience, I didn't have many problems while I was in committed relationships.

Of course there were things that could've been better, but that is a part of life. Things happen, and some relationships just do not work out, and that is okay. Just because a relationship doesn't work out doesn't mean it was a bad experience. We have to be realistic with how we look at relationships. Sometimes, and most of the time, we only interact with certain people to learn from them and to move on. Think about how many people you've met, interacted with, or known. Everyone cannot be your best friend, and everyone cannot be your soul mate, if you believe in that kind of thing. That is just a realistic viewpoint of life. All relationships, regardless of what we think, end at some point, even if that point is death. Realistically, they all end, so expecting forever doesn't even sound realistic.

But that moment had me thinking about my "worth" and if this concept is even real. It also made me think this thought of myself: "Am I acting or thinking like a victim?" I really had to sit and pause and explore this vibration. I wanted to know if I was holding myself back.

Victim Mind-Set—How to Become Self-Aware to Prevent Relationship Suffering

A victim is a person who has been injured, harmed, killed, tricked, or duped via an accident or event (as described by Dictionary.com).

The victim mind-set is the most destructive mind-set a person can have. You feel like the world is out to get you. You feel like nobody is kind, like nobody is happy. You don't believe in real love. You are the type of person who will never be happy at any job because you don't think jobs are fulfilling or rewarding (which really is just a case of poor job alignment). Being a victim allows you to remain pessimistic and doubtful. It allows you remain hurt, jaded, and terrified of moving forward. At no point should you just ignore or not deal with the pain that occurs. Being disconnected from the reality of your experiences is not what I am preaching. Yes, feel the pain; embrace the sorrows of life. Never ignore any feelings that you get, especially while you're experiencing something traumatic. You will get cut from a team, you will lose a job, you will be broken up with, someone will mistreat you, or someone will pick another person over you. This is life. This is realistic. However, you do not and should not internalize the pain of these incidents. They do not have to control you.

You have to go through and deal with life; you're entitled to any negative feelings that come your way. The problem is not feeling them or even expressing them. The true problem arises when you stay there—caught up in your negative feelings—for months and months, because that turns into years and years. Again, this is a very sensitive process, and each person's range of time to heal is different.

How do you create a relationship in the technology generation? The first thing you must do is create an efficient relationship with yourself. Most people get steamrolled and left out of what they want, because they don't really know what they want. Even worse, they don't act with purpose and clarity. Most of us are lost, yet we expect to find love. Love is not something you need to search for—it occurs inside of you, now and forever. Believe that; love is you, and you are love. Don't search. Just be.

How to Identify if You're Acting like a Victim

One hundred percent of people who are currently speaking from the place of "victim" are pessimistic and petty. They are also defensive and constantly in a state of delusion. The first person that comes to mind is a person that I see online all the time. Yes, I can tell a lot about your emotional status based on the comments you leave online. If I make a posts that says, "He is going to love a woman that has his back and builds with him," there will be at least one woman who's been hurt who will say, "Not all" or "Mine didn't." I honestly hold my phone and just shake my head because the pain is all over the screen. That is an extremely petty response, and it shows that this person is speaking from a place of pain. People who are happy, confident, and on a good path don't have time to nitpick little things like that. They will flat out just ignore it if it's not true, or they won't even notice because they're too busy living their lives. This is a small example that can balloon to others, if you just think about it. I don't want to beat a dead horse and give more and more examples. I believe you get this, right?

How to Stop Being/Acting like a Victim

This may take years, so don't force it. Just allow your course to run as it does. Here are some bullet-point tips that can give instant relief to a person who constantly acts like a victim.

- Talk positively about other people regardless of how shitty they are.
- Journal every day about your life. Writing will actually heal you. Writing is a form of coping and thinking critically without pressure.

Become aware of how petty, defensive, or negative you might actually be by observing yourself and asking friends to observe you.

Victim Mind-Set Continued

To be a victim is to be a person who attracts a consistent state of internal suffering. In fact, the internal suffering is so deep and strong that your desire to continue suffering actually manifests into your physical world. There's no benefit in feeling sorry for yourself or blaming others for your journey. At some point, you have to realize that you have to be the creator of your universe. If you act as if someone else is the power, then how can you actually proclaim that you deserve anything? This doesn't make any sense to me. You claim that you deserve a particular way, but then you don't take full accountability. We have to move past this low-vibrational, nonimpactful, and egregious mind-set.

This type of mind-set destroys self, relationships, and everything else. Being a victim is like dropping a nuclear warhead on a budding avocado tree. It's overkill, unnecessary, and redundant. There's nothing glorious about blaming everyone else for your journey. You are responsible for your journey. Not him, not her, not me, not your mom, not your dad, not your boss, not your church, not your team. You are responsible for your story, so while you sit up here and say stuff like, "There are no good men" or "There are no good women," when are you going to realize that you're creating this mind-set? If you say that there are no good men, then you, as a woman, actually believe that about yourself. You're the reason that there are no good men left, because you believe that state of suffering is true.

You have to be kidding me with an illogical statement like this. You're telling me that out of 7.5 billion people, none are able to be compatible enough with you to actually be in a relationship? Just stop it. Don't tell me how much this generation sucks when you are adding to the madness. I command you to stop talking and acting like a victim. Nobody cares. Your universe is a product of your thoughts, your actions, and your moods. You can't unlearn something once you learn it, so what will you do with this? Will you suffer, or will you let go of the nonsense?

The Victim's Prayer

Healing is a choice. Don't stay heartbroken over heartbreak by focusing on the what if's and the maybes. Don't stay jaded, fearful, and broken because of one experience with one person. There is love again, after pain. You may not believe today, but that doesn't change the fact that real love exists. Real love always exists, and don't you ever say that it doesn't. Is it rare? Of course it's rare. It's rare because this society has pointed you to believe in war, destruction, and darkness. This society teaches you to place blame, to watch others' lives, and to compare every little minute detail about your life to the next person. This is why you suffer. Don't compare your life. Don't compare it to an old or future version of yourself. You can be and then create love. Love is a miracle. Love is a blessing that will always find you once you create it. You'll only manifest it once you believe and then take action to create it. These are choices, so what will you decide?

Sit down with yourself. Be real with yourself.

Be accountable.

Don't talk or act like a victim.

Raise your consciousness; rid yourself of toxic mind-sets and behaviors. Look internally for happiness and validation; vibrate at a frequency that gives you an abundance of bliss, not suffering.

—Sylvester McNutt III, "Victim Mind-Set," *Dear Love Life*

Determine Your Worth: Is This a Real Concept?

This is a very interesting concept, and to me, it's just a term that should guide you toward the true energy that your soul is vibrating at. I need you to be realistic and objective when you try to "determine your worth," because this concept isn't actually hard. This shouldn't be a challenging concept at all. It requires no force or changing. It requires you to look at yourself objectively, no matter what. It requires that you look at yourself without judgment or morality. Then and only then will you be able to determine your worth; then and only then will you be able to make realistic outlooks on life. When you ponder on this subject, what I want you to do is look at the correlation of your actions and your thought processes. Some people truly believe in magic, because they expect certain events to occur without actions that will produce these events. And even worse, there are people who do actions that tarnish the ability to create what they claim they want. These people walk around in life largely unaware of their deficiencies. This is why I am commanding that you analyze yourself in an objective way, all the time. You need to be very realistic. If I told you that I wanted to find a wife, but I go out every weekend, get blacked-out drunk, and have sex with random women from the club every weekend, what would you say?

You would say that I, indeed, do not want a wife and that I want to have sex with random women from the club. Again, these behaviors are not right or wrong, but objectively, do they align efficiently? That is the key word—efficient. I asked you to remove moral judgments and to look at this entire book with an open mind from an efficiency standpoint. Logically, if we put together a realistic and objective analysis of those behaviors versus what I am claiming I want, we will find the truth. In psychology, this is called *cognitive dissonance.*

It is when your actions do not align with your thoughts. I do not have a percentage, because it's something that is really hard to measure, but I am willing to bet my next meal that an overwhelming 60 percent of adults ages eighteen to twenty experience a massive amount of cognitive dissonance when it comes to the dating game.

I am basing that number on my professional interactions, personal experiences, and observations. People come to me every day to give them guidance on their missteps when it comes to life and dating. This is the most important concept to begin with because it makes the user reflect internally, and that is where all of the answers live. The answers to all of your questions are intrinsic—they live inside of you, and in most cases we just refuse to accept the answers. The information I just gave you is what I call a skill. People want relationships so bad, and they do not understand that to be efficient in a relationship, you need to have a multitude of skills.

Efficiency—the State or Quality of Being Efficient

Once you start using this word in your vocabulary, everything will improve in your life. From 2012 to 2014 I was using a shipping company that wouldn't allow me to track my own orders for my books. In 2015 my popularity as a writer really started to boom.

I went from getting no e-mails about book orders to hundreds per day, and it was overwhelming. Shipping was not operating as efficiently as it could have been, although at the time it made sense to me.

See, this is why we fail in our relationships. We develop habits, and we think that it works for us because it worked for us at one point in the past. Again, another illogical mind-set that will ruin every single relationship. I had to look at how I was running things, and then I determined that I needed a new system because the current one wasn't efficient. I wanted my customers to get tracking numbers so they knew where their products were at, and most of all I wanted to protect myself as a company. I needed that peace of mind knowing that my customers were going to get their products. What happens if a hundred people say they never received their products? I'm either going to be out of money because I'll have to ship more books, or they'll be without their products because they won't reach out and let me know. Previously, for the lower volume, the process was fine, but as orders increased, it was potentially deadly, so I killed that process and started shipping every book myself. The new shipping process gave a customer a tracking number via e-mail every single time. I had the same access, and I was able to sign damn near every book. This also made the experience more personal and gave me peace of mind that these customers will come back for future projects. At the release of this book, I honestly do not know what procedure I will use, because I am a very popular writer now, and the demand is higher than I am truly ready for. That is a blessing and a curse. I only arrived at this conclusion by using objective-reasoning skills and observing myself without judging myself. I only improved my situation because I was able to admit that I was not operating as efficient as I could be. Most of us don't grow because we don't change once we see a problem. You have to be willing to grow at all times.

Getting the love that you deserve

isn't about what you search for; it's only about what you are, what you give, and what you choose to allow around you. You are always in the process of manifestation. You're the creator of your love life.

—Sylvester McNutt III, *Dear Love Life*

What Is Your Love About?

This isn't a question. It's a rhetorical statement, really. There does not need to be a deep analysis to the question, because you already know the answer. Most of us overshoot and overguess our abilities; we have an illusory perception of our own abilities. I'm not asking you to grade yourself—grading requires that you look at what you did or do wrong, and I never want you to do that again. Looking at yourself as "wrong" is not my goal. This isn't a book about morality. It's about decision making and understanding. I've asked you to suspend morality and open your mind. Ask yourself, no, observe yourself; there's no reason to ask, because you already know the answer.

What is your love about? Do not compare the depth or quality of your love to the next person or to what you have been conditioned to believe love is. The images you see in the media are illusions, only illusions, covered up by lights and shadows. Do not believe what you see in this external world around any format of love, because none of it is real. The real love you claim you want does not exist outside of you. How can it? Logically, please tell me how love, which is an intrinsic occurrence, has the ability to occur outside of you. There is no rational, logical answer that you could give to determine this. We have found an axiom here, and that is that love occurs internally. If you see a beautiful butterfly floating around in the park, you may smile, but the love you have for that butterfly occurred inside of you. Yes, it is an external object, but the feeling didn't occur outside of you. It occurred inside of you, and it always will. However, there really is no separation between you and the butterfly; you two are connected for that moment. See, we get lost in the translation of understanding love because we have been trained via our media and conditioning to think that love is the butterfly.

We have been taught to think that people find love once they find the persons who wants to commit to them and then marry them, and that is not love holistically. We label our worth and say that if we do not have this one type of relationship, then we are not loved, or we are not as valuable as a person who has this. How can this be true? This is prevalent today when you listen to women who are around they age of thirty talk about how they should be married with kids and a house.

Who is teaching them that this is a realistic expectation? When will we learn that seeking and searching is the root of unhappiness? You do not have that love, because you are not that love. You cannot find something that you already own. Your mission is to be the type of love that you desire, but we've been brainwashed to think that something external can somehow validate an intrinsic quality that is already inside of each of us. The only mission here is to accept and understand that love occurs inside of you, me, and every other human being now and forever and that there is no value to go on a search for it, but the true value is to build what is already inside of you organically. The next butterfly you see will be just as beautiful, and it isn't because the color pigments match your idea of beauty. It is because that love already lives inside of you. So objectively, you need to ask yourself, "What is my love about?" and then you can observe yourself as you are and take a realistic inventory of who you are. I feel that, as of today, January 8, 2016, I am full of love and life. I have a light that illuminates energy that attracts the best out of other people. My light brings out efficient behaviors in most of the people I am around. My friends naturally challenge themselves to improve and grow in different pillars of life.

My presence enables them to organically introspect without the grading aspect of judgment, but to become aware. Objectively, my love also can feel like pressure to a person who doesn't understand me or my purpose. It's up to me to consciously and effortlessly become aware of myself so I do not sabotage another's ability to exist around me. This is the challenge of bringing consciousness to your relationship. You need to do it, but again, you can only control your own self.

Being mindful of who you are gives you power, and power is how you build efficiency. If you can become aware of your impact, you can navigate the waves of adversity in all relationship matters, so again, what is your love about? Once you accept the depths of that answer, regardless of how toxic or dirty the answer may be, then and only then will you be able to give the most efficient version of your love. There's no good or bad, just a level of efficiency, and that is all you have.

I Command You Not to Have a Type—It Will Hurt You

I wanted to be with her. She was perfect. This girl had the hips of a goddess and the hair of an angel. Her voice was soft and raspy at the same time. Her stomach was flawless, as I remember from many nights kissing her and picturing how my child would one day come from her. She smiled when she saw me and laughed at all my punch-lineless jokes; she made me feel like I was valuable and important.

I have a visual fascination with long hair. I've always been attracted to girls with long hair, even when I was a child watching television shows. Growing up, there was this show named *Boy Meets World*. Depending on your age, you may be very familiar with the character Topanga Lawrence, played by actress Danielle Fishel. As a young boy, she was the very first girl that I truly idolized, lusted after, and desired. In real life, she is only a handful of years older than me, but she was on television, so it gave her an allure; she truly was a beautiful girl, regardless of her job. I am able to look back in retrospect and recognize that seeing her formulated the idea of what a woman should be like for me. She became my type. This happens for all of us. Your opposite-sex parent may become your type too, especially if you actually enjoyed that parent growing up. My mother, a lighter-skinned African American woman from Chicago, Illinois, also represents my type. Exactly half of my relationships have been with women who look just like that. In my specific case, my taste in women became what I saw at home and what I saw on the television screen. This analysis should always be introspective, because everyone is exposed to different environments, stimuli, and situations. Results may vary.

This observation is neither good nor bad —it just is. I believe that since she was one of my first memories, and the memories of her are all associated with happiness, what actually happened is I formulated an unconscious bridge of attraction to her type—my type. At the same time, I became interested in another character named the Pink Ranger on a show called *Mighty Morphin Power Rangers*. I was subjected to this media, and thus it helped formulate an ideal *type*. If I had to describe my ideal type from an attraction-only perspective, it would be a dark-haired girl with medium-long to long hair. She would be leaner and have an athletic build. Again, we are just looking objectively at ourselves, and I urge you to do the same thing for yourself. Now, what happens is we start to do this for all the pillars of dating. As far as personality and communication go, both

ters were extremely kind, passionate, and
Vhat type of character traits do you think I
or in women? Developing a type is
lly normal, but don't become closed
minded. It's very possible and highly likely that
in this dating landscape, we must be open to
ideas that are uncomfortable.

Different pillars can be the ones used
here, which are attractiveness, communicative
abilities, sense of humor, and ability to cope with
stress. Once we choose pillars, we develop
something called a *type*. Having a type is where
the majority of us, in this generation, go
completely wrong, in the sense of our abilities to
be efficient. If you really think about what a type
is, it is just a story or a marginalized box of
thinking that you're using to control you.
Friends, I've said it before, and I'll say it again,
but what makes us think we have this ability to
control everything? When will we realize that
our obsession with control is what will leave us
lonely, bitter, and upset? At what point do we
pay attention to the correlation between our
loneliness (and need for attachment) and its
relationship with control? What happens over
time is we develop these types, and they destroy
our abilities to accept everyone as they are. In
my last book, *Dear Soul*, I talked about the
importance of acceptance, and I went on to

explain that the only way to get over any type of pain is to find peace inside of acceptance.

Mankind needs human connections, deep human connections, to feel happy. This statement is backed by science, by consciousness, and by psychologists. We literally need each other, but the worst thing you can do as a human is live in a lane away from acceptance. You need love. You need to accept other humans as they are, without the damnation of your fantasies and illusory thoughts of how they should be, and this is why having a type robs you of that ability.

No, I would never recommend staying in situations of direct abuse. I would never tell you to accept something so vile and disrespectful. I am talking to the large majority of us who have a sense of entitlement, the people who allow unrealistic expectations to dominate their baseline of behaviors. Now and forever, we have to let go of these fantasies, and we have to start accepting each other as we are, or we will continue this plateau of confusion that plummets our happiness. Remain open minded.

I don't want a perfect relationship, just a healthy one where we laugh at each other for no reason. The kind where we people watch and make fun of other couples. It's real love when you can walk down the street and pick out each other's type, knowing you're the only ones for each other.

A "perfect" love is an unrealistic expectation. Things get rough sometimes. I just want a "worth it" love—someone who will stick it through. Just you and I until the sun stops risings in the east.

—Sylvester McNutt III

Chapter 5

How to Identify a

Toxic Relationship,

Person, or Situation

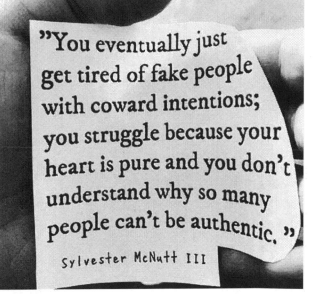

"You eventually just get tired of fake people with coward intentions; you struggle because your heart is pure and you don't understand why so many people can't be authentic."

Sylvester McNutt III

There's a clear distinct and obvious difference between being with someone who wants to be with you and fighting an uphill battle that you can't win. If a lover truly wants you, effort will be put in, even if resources are reduced.. Nothing is perfect, and we all falter in relationships, but effort is the most important pillar. A lover who doesn't try is a lover who doesn't want things to work out. It's possible that a lack of effort is related to a lack of skills. Maybe the two of you need more skills before the partnership can continue. Some say that "Men want a chase." No, let's correct that. Men like a challenge, just like women like challenge. We all do. However, running form a lover who doesn't want to be caught by you is hell on earth and burns your feet like walking across an acid lake. Yes, put up a friendly and competitive challenge, but to chase? No, there's no chasing. Nobody has time to give all of his or her effort to the ghost of someone's yesterday. Be the type of lover who will embrace, hold, and let a person know that their efforts are worth it or not. If you don't like someone, won't like someone, then don't waste his or her time. Allow that individual to give all of that effort to a person who really wants it. Allow him or her to go chase someone who is going to chase back—mutual effort. Don't be the type of person who allows someone to chase you when you have no intention of even considering being with him or her. That's not fair; you're keeping that person around just because your ego likes the attention.

One of the first red flags that you have to identify in terms of dating is people who force you to chase them. I've been in many relationships and one extremely healthy one. Yes, I found her. I pursued her, but she reciprocated the energy and effort from day one and now I have the healthiest relationship that I've ever had. As I sit her and think about the women that made me go above and beyond, they never met me up there. I was their alone, feeding ego, and providing relationship benefits without a commitment. Your first lesson in terms of identifying a red flag and a person who may eventual manipulate you for their guiding is to pay attention to mutual effort. Are you chasing are you being met somewhere int he middle?

You'll go mad trying to chase a lover who does not want to be caught by your hands. Real love doesn't run from its home.

- Sylvester McNutt III, *Dear Love Life*

Let's Talk About Manipulation and The Tactics Used

When you're being manipulated, you never actually know it until it's too late. Manipulation is like being on an airplane. If the plane is going five hundred miles per hour, so are you, but you're not in control. You're at the mercy of the pilot, the wind, and the aircraft. Manipulative people operate as the pilot, the plane, and the wind. Be very careful where you decided to book tickets. It might be a one-way trip to the abyss of manipulation. We all use manipulation tactics throughout relationships; in fact, it's normal. However, some manipulation can be rooted in evil, and that is what we want to avoid. Some manipulation can be innocent and harmless, and other types can destroy self-esteem, pride, and families. It's important that we become aware of such tactics so we can avoid toxic people, but importantly so we can avoid the toxic behaviors. I'm willing to bet that most people, based on their desires, would like to be good but lack skills, which prohibits us from being as pure as we could be. If you read this section and discover that someone you're dating is manipulative at his or her core, don't attack that person, because it's possible that he or she is unaware of it. You care about your partner. Use this information wisely; use this information to improve your current situation and to avoid toxic relationships in the future.

Here, I want to define toxic. Some people believe that just because there's a problem, a difference of opinion, or opposing ideas, these are toxic. No, these are just conflicts. Toxic takes on different, darker elements—bizarre and deranged elements that destroy the relationship's ability to prosper. A toxic situation, environment, or person is one that is extremely harsh, malicious, or harmful.

The Comeback Trail Explained

The very first situation that needs to be talked about is the Comeback Trail. At one point, he (or she) was in your life. Maybe you two were dating. Maybe you were officially together and broke up for some reason. Maybe he's a person that you don't really know, but you guys had a spark, and it died down for some reason. The point that I want you to fully understand is that no matter what, good has been created. But if there is separation, a void has also been created.

A void is a break in presence or communication. It's an absence from your life.

Here the deal. Just because you stop talking to someone, you break up, or he moves away doesn't mean that you stop caring about him. There are two tactics common in our generation based around this theme that need to be discussed. It's vital that you can identify these situations before you get into them. This information will save you years of confusion and conflict.

The first is what I called call "I-miss-you Land," and the second is what I call "shadowing."

I'd like to be as objective as possible for this next line because it truly can be observed in many ways. I'll allow you to decide the message how you wish. First, while using the word *manipulation*, I don't feel like all manipulation is inherently bad or inefficient. Coming from a genuine, loving, and caring person, if you say the phrase "I miss you," it's a form of manipulation. This is such a tough message to truly accept because we all have negative perceptions of the word *manipulation*. That's why we're going to struggle accepting this concept, but let's explore from a perspective of causation. If I have genuine intentions and feelings for you, and I say that "I miss you," I could be speaking directly from my core. However, the motive to express such a mood is generated from self, from a place of benefit. It truly does benefit you when you express to another that you miss him.

Why? Because you're playing to his ego, empowering his vanity and spirit. You're the chess master, and you just moved a pawn forward; you have him in the palm of your hand. Here's the demarcation point. Some, and I'll even say most, people will say a phrase like "I miss you" because they genuinely feel it and want to express it.

But you have to be cautious of the manipulators who understand that you're the perfect target. They know that you're nothing but a passenger in their airplanes. They know that they can tickle your fancy with praise, a little attention, and some newfound consistency. In most cases, nobody is going to ignore such a genuine attempt at expression. But here's the deal. There are two people who use this phrase. A person who genuinely misses you and a person who misses whatever it is you used to do for them. As the perfect target, it is your job to become a master of introspection. It is beyond vital that you understand exactly what people gain from your presence.

I want to give you a hypothetical, and I will parse it so you see where I'm going. This is about taking the power away from manipulative people and understanding them. It's crucial that we understand these modern-day tactics so we can avoid them and, even more importantly, stop being this type of person.

Hypothetical: There's a person that you previously, dated but she (or he) never gave you relationship effort. She got sex, money, and inconsistent communication from you. Maybe it felt like she only contacted you when she needed something.

Let's just all pretend that we were in this situation. Manipulation is about leverage. Think about it like this: Do you remember those teeter-totter machines on the playgrounds—the ones that required two people to work? One person pushed off of the ground and went up. Meanwhile, the other person went down. I want you to view manipulation like that.

You are just minding your business, sitting on this teeter-totter by yourself. Therefore, you're on the ground, and the other end is up in the air. You're in a casual dating situation that never processes to a relationship because of a lack of interest and effort. So here's the deal. We know that if you're reading this book, you care about love. You care about dating. You take your relationships serious because you want to get a great deal of value out of them. There's not a single person who will read this book who just wants sex and toxic situations. I'm willing to bet that you believe in commitment and loyalty, and you feel everything so deeply that sometimes you don't even know how to express yourself. If this is you, then I urge you—no, I command you—not to settle for a manipulator's bullshit.

There's been a void, so she activates the Comeback Trail with an "I miss you" text.

I don't want to use much profanity in this book, but this is a subject I'm truly passionate about. My response to that maneuver is, "Fuck that, and fuck you."

Harsh, I know, but let's keep parsing this. Again, please understand that there is nothing wrong with saying "I miss you." If it's truly genuine and from the fire, a highly intuitive and aware person will know, and it won't be a big deal. However, you're sitting there, on your teeter-totter of life, and she drops the boulder of "I miss you" land on the other seat, skyrocketing you up into a position where you're suspended in the air, looking at her.

The second you respond to this, she now controls you like putty in her hands.

You'll say "Thanks" or "What do you miss?"

And she'll text you back something like this: "I just miss how we used to sit up and talk. I miss our bond. The way you would make me feel."

Stop. Put down your cell phone immediately, and do not respond to that. The person is about to cause you a year of stress. As genuine as this could be, it is *your* duty to make those genuine feelings come out in a genuine way. To date efficiently, we have to use our tools efficiently. Texting is easy. It's effortless. If you're trying to tell me something from your soul, I command you to do it in the most genuine way. You will tell me face to face, you will handwrite or type me a letter, or you will video chat or use the regular phone feature. Under no circumstances will I allow you to manipulate me over texting. I can't hear your voice, your tone, or feel your passion. If you're reading this book, you are just like me. The vibe and energy is everything for you. Therefore, I command you to adopt this requirement for yourself. If a person wants to give you possibly life-changing information over text, implore him or her to stop. It is your duty to create this type of environment for yourself—otherwise they'll destroy you again and again and again.

The Comeback Trail doesn't mean the person is going to ruin you if allow her or him back in. It means that you need to be aware, observant, and conscious. It means that you need to use discernment with your love life. This entire section is only here to give you power, insight, and perspective so your discernment can be top tier.

Let's get specific and talk about manipulation and manipulation over text message. Again, I'm only telling you this information because I don't want you to be ignorant. We can correct a lack of information.

It's 2016, and as a core group of tools, social media and text messaging has been around for less than a decade. But now social media is well implanted into our lives, and multiple generations have transitioned into texting consistently.

This book is ahead of its time because it's addressing the *now*. It's giving insight and strategy into the *now*. Other than basic psychology, all books on dating and relationships are now outdated, and here's why— we are literally in the middle of a paradigm shift. We're not truly aware of this, but we are the guinea pigs, if you will, for this transition and rapid change of human interaction. Obviously, your age matters for your perspective, but anyone who is thirty years or older "remembers a time." He remembers when he had to call a girl's house phone and ask for her from one of her parents. He remembers when commitment meant that you're not sliding into private messages on social media accounts when there's relationship trouble. She remembers when divorce and breaking up were last resorts, not something you do when you don't get your way. Is this to allude that people thirty and under are bad or don't know real love? No, I would never consciously say that. What I can say is that the entire landscape of dating and relationships is changing. We are changing as a species, and that makes sense. We have advanced technological tools that weren't available before. We have created a fast and up-tempo world. We *all* expect everything to happen quickly, and if it doesn't, we move on because we think the grass is greener elsewhere.

In fact, if you ordered this book online, I bet you felt like you deserved or were entitled to a tracking number. I bet you obsessively thought about receiving the book instantly. Why? Because you "deserve" to get it right away? You send texts, and if the recipients don't respond in ten minutes, you assume they don't care. Especially if they're on their phones a lot around you. That logic is flawed, and nobody owes you any response in any timely fashion. However, some want it right away, and this type of "I deserve" entitlement pushes us further and further away from accepting the slow process of building a relationship. You cannot just get married overnight. You cannot create a relationship that is worthwhile overnight. You have to invest every single day for years before it's going to be ready to last forever.

There is no perfect love story. Mine isn't perfect, but what makes my relationship awesome is the fact that she won't quit and give up if she doesn't get her way. She's learned to grow with me and accept me. She has completely followed my lead and allowed me to slow down the dating process. As a man, it's my perception that I should lead the path of the relationship. As much as I agree and actually live this way, I also have to deny it. I can't accept this as a blanket statement: "It's the man's job to lead." See, gender roles and behaviors are changing globally. This is another aspect of the paradigm shift that this book is detailing. If you've actually been in a relationship and are a sensible adult, you'll agree with this statement: in a relationship, nothing is perfect. There are moments where one person picks up the slack for another. There's times where one person has better ideas, systems, or thoughts to increase the happiness in the relationship. The best part of building a worthwhile relationship is the bonding; it's when two become one. Now, there's never going to be a relationship where the woman or man is going to lead all of the time. A true and efficient relationship is one where both partners have enough skills and know-how to at least try to pick up the slack if the other person got sick or wasn't able to lead. In my relationship, she does the laundry, but if she ever gets sick or can't handle it, I will be there to pick up her slack. I try to clean the house, but I can't do it anywhere near as thoroughly as she can. I'm still trying to figure out how she can clean so well. She picks up my slack there. I get the food. I go grocery shopping. I suggest what we should eat. I make sure she has all the tools she needs. I drive everywhere we go. Building a relationship like this takes time.

I need to change your perspective on "men should lead." Please allow me to add a little shock value. In an overwhelming vast majority of men, we are not going to meet you and say, "I'm going to lead this woman to marriage." When we meet you, we are thinking about what you look like in the bedroom. We fantasize over whatever we like about you physically. We're trying to flirt and test you to see how far you'll allow us to go. Even a relationship-minded man still wants sex. It's in his biology. So if your mind-set is "I want to develop a committed relationship," allowing only the man to lead is going to lead you to a sloppy blow job in his living room. Which we are not against, but most men need more than just sex to commit. A man needs a woman to lead, to show him that being in a committed relationship with her will be the greatest decision he ever made. As much as I love the idea of a man courting a woman, we can't act so naive and believe that this only goes one way. In fact, women are always competing and trying to prove their worth to guys. This already happens, but we don't acknowledge it. As a father, I will never teach my daughter that her job is to take a passive role in her love life and just allow a man to lead her into the abyss of whatever he wants.

Why does anyone believe that a man you don't know should be given the keys to your heart? This is not a logical conclusion at all.

If you read this objectively, you'll see that the author is missing one word. Are you ready? Balance. No, I didn't say equal. Nothing is fair or equal in life. I'm saying balance. Don't seek for the path to occur any specific way.

Balanced Love

In terms of efficiency, the most important thing you can do is find a constant of balance. Men and women we are made to counter each other. You have to push and pull; you have to lead and follow; you have to submit and be a person worth submitting to; you have to communicate, invest, and put the other person first. A truly balanced love is one where two people invest in each other so much that they understand where to pick the other person up at. We are in a paradigm shift. Do not reduce your relationship to just a gender expectation that someone else made for you. Once you're actually in the relationship, the gender roles do not matter. Why? Because you've formed a conglomerate based one two people, not what society or some book is telling you to do.

I've seen my best friend be a stay-at-home dad because his wife's job made more money. I watched him and his wife switch roles a year later. If they would've just went with what society says, they would've been homeless. Gender roles truly matter in the beginning because people don't know each other, and they're trying to mold a life. As you grow, the roles morph into something based on the two participating parties.

Women Who Text All Day Are Easy to F*** Over

I highly recommend you go to YouTube right now and watch the ten-minute video I did on this topic. You can simply search exactly what this title says: "Women Who Text All Day Are Easy to F*** Over." Earlier we were talking about manipulation, and if you rely on texting as a primary form of communication, then you are an easy victim, especially to a person who understands power and psychology. Men do practice lazy dating techniques when they're allowed to. They truly enjoy what I call "the path of least resistance."

Logic: *You're right. I don't need to ask you on a date, because you don't require it. I really don't need to call you, because you're okay with inconsistent communication. You allow me to jump in and out of your life as I wish, because you do not require more than that. The truth is, I do not lack integrity, so you* *cannot blame me and say that I am doing something wrong. I am only participating in the madness that you allow.* Women are emotionally connected to words, so texting you is easy to him because most women will attach their subjective, emotional viewpoints to the conversation. Men, typically more logical, use texting to relay information. That is the key difference that I see in generalizations of gender uses with texting. Women use text to express, and men use it to relay information. All of time? Of course not—it's just a very common generalization.

Text messaging all day is not an authentic form of communication. I want to present you the two common errors that I see women making in dating. Yes, men make these same mistakes, but from my trials, clients, and observations, women are much more probable to experience this. It can be innocent or done as manipulation. I don't want you to suffer, so here it is:

Text Message Screening

Some women truly feel like they can make themselves feel safe and more at ease by screening a guy on social media or through text messaging. Women are smart. Actually, the modern-day woman is a part-time private investigator. Somehow, women just know how to get information.

Men have been trying to figure this out for decades, but we'll never know. As powerful as their reasoning and observation skills are, nothing, and I mean nothing, compares to a man who knows psychology, seduction, and charm. No woman can match a guy who knows all three. He has the ability to break every single wall she has, while feeling like he's known her for years. This type of man is actually on the rise for one main reason—women participate and promote "text message screening."

This is the idea that they'll prod, ask questions, and penetrate the fortress of who he might be. Women fall into this trap because they actually reveal *all* of the information that he needs to know to either wife them or destroy them. It's the same information, built on his path and desire. See, when you give a man of substance information, he uses it to position you wherever he wants.

Yes, it's a form of manipulation, but it's not necessary negative. In fact, it's needed. It's a part of the process of getting to know each other, and he naturally wants to find out whatever he can so he can put her in the most comfortable situation possible. At the root of what the word *manipulation* means, this is manipulation. This is such a slippery slope and catch-22 because this screening, in my mind, should occur in person and through conversation as often as possible. It's natural and healthy, but herein lies the problem. Women are giving out all of the information that helps them break their walls down over text message. Now, his response can be genuine, calculated, or absent. Either way, she's already tricked herself into feeling fake comfortable.

Text Message Deception

The deception happens next. If a man is newly dating, I'm willing to bet nine times out of ten he is trying to have sex with her. As a man, we want to test the pussy and see how it feels. Please refer to the dating table that I gave earlier to understand what type of dater you may be dealing with.

It's imperative, that as a woman, you have sex under conditions that you have deemed okay. Why? Please visit the "Friends with Benefits Introspection" section, where I break down the biological and chemical differences for sex. In most cases, a woman can trick a man into sex, and he won't feel bad about it. It feels unnatural to turn down sex. He wants sex, so you can't really trick him. Sex does not equate to love for him, but it does equate to his at-the-moment activity. Like I said earlier, sex for a woman can literally make her fall in love. These are not emotions to be played with.

If you're going to date, you're going to have sex, and you're going share intimate space with people in the name of getting to know them. It is your duty and obligation to reveal private, sacred, and intimate information face to face so you can intuitively judge your sexual partners accordingly. Now, in this generation, all you have to do as a guy is text several women all day, and you can have a roster of women who are ready to have sex with you. It is the easiest it's ever been for that because women truly do require less than before. Texting is easy.

Women, I challenge you to require men to call you as the primary form of communication. I also challenge you to require yourself to call him too. He is *not* going to call you if you text all day. He has no reason to. You've set the bar that all we have to do is text. Pick up the phone and call so you can guarantee authentic exchanges.

Over text, all he has to do is transform into the "right" guy so he can be the guy you want to have sex with later. In real life, you can transform into that if you are that. In a real-life interaction, you can never transform into someone who you are not.

You're a different type of human. You read books, your energy transcends and uplifts. You're known to put your passion into everything that you do. You've graduated from playing text message games with little boys who don't have the confidence to call you and stir up a deep, authentic conversation. You demand more because you give more. You'll call him too. You'll write him letters and dedicate your time to focus on building with you. At this point, you're not going to play second fiddle to anyone's casual text messages. Your *Dear Love Life* deserves more than a "Hey, what you doin'?" You're looking for something real and deep. The shallow, weak connections have officially been abolished.

—Sylvester McNutt III, *Dear Love Life*

In a nourishing, sensible, and superlative relationship, you become each other's safe haven. The amalgamation of your energy and the other person's splashes together to make a rainbow of pleasure. In a healthy relationship, the two people sacrifice manipulation and control techniques. When you truly love someone, you don't seek to control them; your only goal is to move silently with his or her soul across this plane of life, together. Real love is a magical trip, like two kids who skipped through a meadow, laughing, playing, and rhythmically manifesting ecstasy.

—Sylvester McNutt III, "Real Love"

Toxic people have a special set of skills; they make wrong feel right and hell feel like a home that you should lie down in. Toxic people know how to make you forget that they are the monsters that keep you up at night. They mask your judgment with lies, manipulation, and deceit, but they make it feel so warm and dandy.

—Sylvester McNutt III,

"Manipulation Tactics"

Dear Love Life

Manipulation Tactics That Destroy the Effective Relationship-Building Process

Gaslighting

People use this technique to make you insecure or crazy or irrational in your process. They'll put you down, call you names, and say things like "You're crazy." This technique is used for positioning, for leverage, for control, and for power. Remember, that gas-lighting is the process of destroying your reality. This tactic is about making your perception of the world or event smaller and irrelevant. This is why people will ask for credentials when you're presenting information, or maybe they'll speak on that one-off occurrence when something spectacular happened, just to prove you wrong. A gaslighter's main goal is to be right and to prove to you that he (or she) is right by any means necessary. He will use big words, emotional slippery slopes, and any type of mental jarring to get you to bow down. You're easily susceptible to a gaslight experience if you don't have your own version of the truth. At some point, you have to have a backbone, and you have to understand that some things are not open to reality change. Nobody can tell you how to feel. Yes, poets can describe your feeling, but nobody can discredit and throw out your feelings. If you say that you're feeling unappreciated, then that is your feeling. You're allowed to own that. If we're dating, and I tell you that you shouldn't feel that way, I am dead wrong. I am gaslighting you. This is black and white; you're allowed to have your own thoughts, feelings, and beliefs. You can easily stop gaslighting by not participating. Like I mentioned earlier, nobody has to be right. It's perfectly okay to share different perspectives on an idea. I observe that a lot of unhealthy relationships struggle and fight because one partner thinks that the other person has to agree with him or her. Friends, nobody has to be right, ever, actually. You can take the time to listen and just empathize with another person, even if you disagree. You never have to be right, ever. You will suffer greatly if you seek the ability to be right, to have a point proven, or to gain approval of self. Also, accept that you may be wrong. There's no reason to react to every little bit of conflict. Learn how to let things go. Gaslighting happens because people hold on to a position in the conversation instead of just being a participant.

**You will continue to suffer If you have an emotional reaction
To everything that is said to you.
True power is sitting back and Observing everything with logic;
Power is restraint. If words always control you, that
Means everyone else can control you;
Breathe and allow things to pass.**

—Sylvester McNutt III, *Dear Love Life*

Silent Treatment

A passive way to control behavior. People act silent and ignore you to rile you up since they're now exuding a new behavior. Their lack of action, communication, or expression is causing you to try to pick up the slack and do more because of the feeling to compensate. People use silent treatment because they're angry or because they want to punish the other person. Silent treatment tactics involve ignoring texts, not retuning phone calls, and even telling a person, "I'm not talking to you right now." The tactic often causes the users to create this narcissistic entitlement as they pump their egos with self-serving statements like, "They don't deserve to talk to me." Silent treatment is often used after a breach of trust. Objectively, it makes sense. You don't want to talk to you partner because he hurt you. That feeling makes a lot of sense; however, not communicating, especially in a time of crisis, is creating more suffering and more stress. I highly recommend that you never, ever hit someone with the silent treatment. If you're trying to break up and move on from a lover, then a no-contact situation makes sense. The most effective way to do that is to communicate that there will be no communication moving forward. Yes, this is hard to do, but it does give closure to both parties. In cases of physical abuse, I do not recommend initiating contact. Sometimes the only option is to go silent and go away. That makes sense.

Blame Shifting

The best manipulators know exactly how to make you feel bad for the same behavior. I can leave my dirty towels everywhere, but you can't? These people truly focus on the double standard because it's all about control and exception to them. They also shift blame when conflict arises. If you listen to superstar athletes after they lose, what do they speak about? They say things like, "We just have to get better and play better defense." The really bold ones that hold a lot of power will say things like, "It was my fault. I have to do a better job of getting my teammates involved and helping them get more opportunity to score." If you're prideful, it's very hard to give credit in the face of defeat, but these types of statements say a lot about someone's character: "I want to give a shout out to that team we just played. They played hard. They were coached well, and they deserved the victory tonight." All of those are healthy statements, and they give credit, or they accept responsibility for the outcome. Blame shifting is the opposite; it points fingers and blames another person every time something goes wrong. A blame shifter always tells you that you're not good enough or how you are the problem or the reason. Everything is your fault.

Guilt Trip

"I told you so." They try to make you feel bad for a misstep or poor decision by reminding you about it often. Especially if they presented you another option. They'll try to gain power by telling you that you need to listen to them because their way is the right way. Guilt trippers don't actually respect your decisions or consciousness. They attack your decision-making ability by spending time convincing you of another answer. Your consciousness and experience is not as important as theirs; to them, it's all about the final outcome from their perspective. Guilt trips happen often, and it's important to note that they occur in close relationships. It's highly unlikely that we will guilt trip a person that really is indifferent about us. We can only trip those who choose to stand with us. Guilt tripping can occur in a playful manner and it is not harmful like that. However, if it is being used consistently to control he other person, especially if they are an empathic person, then this is very dangerous. Since an empathy feels everything so deep the guilt tripper uses this to their advantage to control their every step.

Physical Coercion

They use violence or threats of violence to control and manipulate situations. This should never occur. There is no room for violence in relationships. Nobody should ever attack another person that you claim you love. Violence is for self-defense and survival, not to express yourself in matters of dating. If you truly cannot communicate without breaking household items, exerting violence (or the threat of violence), I encourage you to seek help. That is anger. Anger can lead people to do things that will destroy families and lives. Don't let anger keep you trapped in a vicious cycle. I've gone on record to state that I do not believe violence is a healthy part of any relationship. I do not believe in having abuse between me and my child or me and my children. After dedicating 120 hours to understanding violence and the psychological impact of violence, I have determined that violence is a zero-tolerance policy in relationships. I was abused as child and watched domestic violence in my house until I was old enough to yell at my parents to stop. I have never hit a woman or child that I loved, and I never will. Violence has physiological markings that ruin a person's ability to remain pure and happy. Because of classical conditioning, I don't want anyone I love to connect my face to the art of violence. I am a lover. I am here to love; I do not have the emotions, the time, or the desire to spread hate to anyone. Therefore, the act of violence, which is a hate crime to me, cannot live in any loving relationship that I have.

In fact, my good friend just reached out to me yesterday morning, and I am going to tell you what I told her. She told me that she thought she took her last breath because her ex hit her in the face with a bottle and choked her until she no longer could tell him to get off of her. I cried all morning after I read this text. I wanted to hold her, to let her know that it was okay. I wanted her to know that just because she is experiencing domestic violence, it doesn't have to be that way. I wanted her to know that she wasn't alone and that if she couldn't talk to her family about it, there are always professionals ready to help out.

I told her that most victims of abuse feel helpless; they feel lost and like it is their fault. They have Stockholm syndrome and often make excuses for their abusers. People who accept domestic violence often do not see a way out. They think that all men or women are going to be like this, so why leave? Their reality has been marginalized and compacted to believe that they deserve this, but they don't, because nobody deserves violence whenever love is there. The last thing I told her was that she needed to report it. I am a strong believer that all violent occurrences need to be reported. I want to say that violence only gets worse as time goes on, and as the bond gets deeper, the violence gets stranger. Yes, in some cases, the violence will stop. But I do not believe in playing those odds.

You can tell that from my personal experience, education, and life experiences, I have seen more than enough of this to feel passionately enough about it, to risk placing this in my book. In conclusion, I believe that all humans should keep violence out of their quality relationships, ones that contain compassion and vulnerability and love. Yes, I know some humans feel that violence is necessary, and I do agree that in times of survival, you have to do what has to be done to protect yourself. Violence is not needed in the home, in your heart, or on the skin of someone you love.

Unfair Fighting

I hate to use this situation, but we see it all the time, and it bothers me. In high school you see kids who aren't mentally challenged make fun of the mentally challenged kids. A famous celebrity is in hot water right now because he was making fun of a kid with autism, claiming that he smoked too much and that this behavior is a part of the generation. The celebrity poked fun at this kid with autism. and it seemed to be an unfair fight, from my perspective. It's highly possible that he didn't know, but that's not my call to judge. All I can do is notice the unfair fight. Just like the twelfth grader who picks on the ninth grader. That person is physical and mentally more advanced, yet he is so weak and insecure that he has to pick on a person who is not on his level. This also happens in relationships in the way that we argue. Conflict is a huge part of relationships, but it doesn't have to destroy them. You can go years and years without having a huge argument. Unfair fighting will always lead to other problems: calling names, swearing, and becoming extremely aggressive—all unfair. Making fun of others for something they can't control is not fair. It's unfair to guilt trip people to change something that they simply cannot change. It's unfair to make people fight battles alone that they cannot win, and then you throw it in their faces. Using phrases like "I told you so" is unfair. People make mistakes. People give bad information at times, and that is okay, but don't rub in how wrong a person was. Saying things like "You're not enough of this or enough of that" or "You're too much of this or too little or that" are all phrases that can allude to unfair fighting. These statements need to be fair at all times. If I wanted to apply to be a scientist and you said, "Sylvester, you don't have the educational background to be a scientist today. You'll need to go back to school," we can say that this is a fair statement. It's based on facts. I don't have the education to support me if I wanted to be a scientist. If you find yourself telling people what they cannot do or who they cannot be, make sure that it is factual, and understand that your facts still might not be true.

Stonewalling

This behavior will typically lead to a breakup or divorce. Stonewalling will lead to resentment, to a person who feels the need to cheat, and to a person who constantly pushes a partner away. Stonewalling is a closed minded "I don't want to talk about it" or "We will talk when

I'm ready" manipulation. Oftentimes, the root is anger or resentment, so the person who feels that wants to push away the other person.

John Gottman is a mastermind and genius with predicting divorce. Here are his thoughts on stonewalling, from his book *The Seven Principles for Making Marriage Work* (Harmony, 2015):

> Stonewalling occurs when the listener withdraws from the interaction. The antidote is to practice physiological self-soothing. The first step of physiological self-soothing is to stop the conflict discussion. If you keep going, you'll find yourself exploding at your partner or imploding (stonewalling), neither of which will get you anywhere. The only reasonable strategy, therefore, is to let your partner know that you're feeling flooded and need to take a break. That break should last at least twenty minutes, since it will be that long before your body physiologically calms down. It's crucial that during this time you avoid thoughts of righteous indignation ("I don't

have to take this anymore") and innocent victimhood ("Why is he always picking on me?"). Spend your time doing something soothing and distracting, like listening to music or exercising.

In one of our longitudinal research studies, we interrupted couples after fifteen minutes and told them we needed to adjust the equipment. We asked them not to talk about their issue, but just to read magazines for half an hour. When they started talking about their issue again, their heart rates were significantly lower and their interaction more positive and productive.

It's imperative that each person takes the time needed to work through anger. However, it is important that you do not go to sleep without talking about it. A person who stonewalls often holds it in for days, weeks, and months that she (or he) is upset, and then she'll blow up at you and still refuse to actually talk about it. She feels like you should've known and that you should just "get it." I don't teach that in my writings. Nobody should just "get it." The only thing we should get is what is communicated to us verbally and nonverbally, and with intent. I truly believe that the more you communicate, the more intuition and empathy can increase. It's easier to "just get" someone once you have communicated with that person so many times. However, it's still not an excuse to have this as an expectation. Nobody can read minds, so deal with your anger, and then communicate. Do not go to bed angry and disgusted because you guys didn't talk. Happy couples look for solutions quickly. In fact, happy couples learn to let many things go before they even became a bigger issue.

Character Flaws Lead to Unproductive Mind-Sets—There's no getting around it. Some people just have flawed characters and unproductive mind-sets, which lead to these kind of statements: "I'm not changing" and "I am unapologetic" and "If you can't take me at my worst..." These people exude behaviors that destroy efficient relationship building. They are often "too much" of any one thing, and I don't care what these corny relationship writers tell you—the truth is, if you are bringing a destructive behavior to a relationship and then justifying it by saying, "Well, that's just how I am," please understand that this is stonewalling, and stop it now. This is a manipulation tactic that people use to force other people to minimalize their value systems, desires, or compatibilities. Oftentimes, they'll appease you because you're using a manipulation tactic. Manipulation is about power. Weaker-minded people will typically just roll with this type of nonsense because they don't have the psychological awareness to understand the irrationality behind these statements. I know what you're thinking, and stop that. You're thinking about how I've said over and over that love is about acceptance and that if they're trying to change you, they don't love you.

Yes, I have said that, but this paragraph is premised with one key difference. If you're doing something that is clearly toxic, dysfunctional, or inefficient and then demanding that another person submit, that is manipulation, and that is not fair. You are pushing that person into a corner. Why can't you accept that you have character flaws that ruin relationships too?

Be grateful that you have a person who is actually trying to communicate with you. Be grateful that he she (or he) is bold enough to risk hurting herself by telling you about herself. She took a big risk, and you're shitting all over a person that you care about by saying, "If you can't accept me at my worst, then you don't deserve me at my best." Stop it, and understand that she shouldn't accept you. If she's a real partner, you better believe she's going to be there trying to push you, to motivate you, or to get you to a different level. That sounds like real love to me.

That sounds like a person who wants to be there with you while you're at your best too. In fact, it feels like she's trying to raise your vibrational awareness and situation. So tell me why you wouldn't want to change for this person. If I'm not at my best, then dammit, I'm sorry, and please help me. Please do not ever accept me at my worst. I do not want a love like that. I need someone who wants me to be accountable, impactful, and responsible for my contributions to our relationship. I don't care if I just met you or if we've been together for a decade. I do not want you at your worst. When you reach your worst, that means we both failed each other, and it's time to rebuild, with each other, from scratch, because that's real love.

One of the highest forms of human communication is to admit fault. We sit on our bubbles and feel like we can do no wrong, but that is when everything falls apart.

Be kinder than you were yesterday. Give more of your soul to help others. Always remain modest and accountable for yourself. If you want to have a consistent format of conflict resolution in your relationship, always be accountable.

—Sylvester McNutt III, "Conflict Resolution—the Key to All Relationship Suffering," *Dear Love Life*

People who knowingly manipulate you just so they can benefit and so you can suffer do not deserve your love. When you truly love someone, you don't manipulate, control, or put that person down. This is not negotiable; this is law. Love does not live inside of these malicious mindsets or behaviors.

—Sylvester McNutt III,
"No Manipulation,"
Dear Love Life

Conflict Resolution—the Key to Ending All Relationship Suffering

Measure Internal Conflict

After everything I've seen, experienced, and studied about relationships, I have to deduce that most problems are intrinsically felt and that they are not felt by both partners. Meaning, it's unfair and unrealistic of me to expect others to feel my pain, to understand why I am upset, or to force them to see it my way. We, as humans, must always seek to find solutions inside of ourselves. The first step to understanding your relationship conflict is to figure out if a problem is a 100 percent purely intrinsic occurrence. I'll give an example of this. Sometimes, we may be blind to what affects others. For example, my girlfriend has been bugging me about getting new knives and pots and pans. For me, based on my awareness and desires, this only impacts her. The ones we have are just fine to me. My perspective is correct. Her perspective is correct. Based on our experiences and desires, neither of us is wrong. However, her desires create a conflict for her, whereas my desire is met because I want it the way it is. She mentioned it once and let it go for a while because it was strictly an internal conflict that she measured. One day, she reached a breaking point and said, "I need your debit card, and we aren't eating off of this stuff anymore." I gave her my card, and she got the utensils that day. Even though it was not my conflict, I had the ability to help her resolve the conflict that she had. At the end of the day, she is happy because it makes the kitchen more domestic, which is something that is important to her value system. She told me that "I'm just a guy, and guys can get by with barely any utensils." I laughed about it and said, "You're right." This could have become something major, but we both handled it in a way that was efficient. We both compromised. She got what she wanted it, but it wasn't right away, and she didn't trick me into doing it. The first time she mentioned it, I let it go because it wasn't a big deal to me or to her. When it became a big deal to her, then it became a big deal to me. Remember, just because something is a big deal to you doesn't mean the other person has to care at the level that you care. Don't get upset if that happens.

When a problem arises, always ask yourself, "Does this only affect me?" Because there are instances where a problem can be squashed without the other person even knowing about it. A few months ago, my lady's energy was off. She wasn't herself. I could feel it, so I asked her what was wrong. Of course, she acted like nothing was wrong, and she just sat and sulked in a chair. I could tell her energy was off, so I asked her again, and then she finally told me that there was a female friend of mine that made her uncomfortable. It's uncomfortable when a new lover has issues with people of the opposite sex, especially the ones who were in your life before your lover. We have a sense of narcissistic entitlement, so we think that people should stay until we feel like they shouldn't be there, but that isn't a fair idea. To be 100 percent transparent, you and I both know that at times we have allowed people to linger in our lives longer than they needed to be there. This girl was a girl who openly expressed her feelings for me, and my new love interest could feel that. My girl's dating style is solo, and mine is playing the field. This was the first time our dating styles clashed. I was dating more than one person, and she was only dating me. I'm sharing this story for two reasons: One, it shows you how two patient adults, with different dating styles, can navigate through dating styles. Second, it shows another way to deal with conflict.

I wasn't 100 percent sure that I wanted to be with her. I spent most of my time with her and put the majority of my energy with her. However, I still had conversations with the other girl. Eventually, since my style is based on a logical choice I realized that it wasn't even a choice at all. I realized that I had fallen in love with her. I loved everything about her, so I told her that I wanted to commit to her and that I wanted to be with her. Her intuition was right at the beginning. I had interest in another girl that I had met before her. When this conflict came up, she didn't give me an ultimatum. She didn't say that I needed to pick her or the other girl. She knew I liked both people. I was honest. She supported me and continued to act in loving ways toward me without holding a grudge. Now, I understand that some daters will just keep both people, if possible. I am not advocating that. I'm only giving you a real-life example of how conflicts in dating can be resolved; they need communication and understanding.

Last thing, always be willing to tell yourself that you're holding on to an outcome or position. Sometimes, we have to let things go. Both people. It's not about picking all of these battles. It's about having a good time, and most of the time, we can do that if we just allow things that truly do not matter to pass by. I'm not telling you not to have a backbone. I know you're tough and smart. I'm advising that you use your best discernment and let go of things that truly do not matter. Insert integrity and maximum belief in your thoughts at all times, but be willing to accept and appreciate opinions, outcomes, and perspectives that do not agree with yours. With love, nobody needs to be right; seek to understand more than you seek to be understood. In a relationship, remember, it's about understanding each other and not trying to prove that you're right. What good does it do you to consistently prove your partner wrong or to put that person down? Uplift your lover and let go of the power-position struggle. Conflict resolution is always more important than the conflict.

Chapter 6

Social Media: The Private Investigator, the Problem Creator, and the Soul Mate Connector

Your relationship with yourself will always be more important than your relationship with your followers and controlled online content.

- *Sylvester McNutt III*

One of the biggest issues that we face in our generation is emotional cheating. We do it more than we realize. In order for us to create the relationships that we truly want, a lot of use need to break up with our cell phones, first.

- *Sylvester McNutt III*

The Salary or
the Relationship

I was a store manager at one of the top telecommunication companies in the world, and I loved my job. I had a sense of pride and accomplishment, largely due to the ranking system and competitive nature that the job offered me—especially since I grew up in sports and played professional football. I found that sales was my calling. Originally, I started doing sales back in Illinois, and that's how I met Dove. Here, I want to give you the backstory so you can grasp how we started. It was so crazy how I met her. I saw her on a mutual friend's Facebook page and told myself that I needed her in my life. I messaged her one night, and of course, she didn't respond. But I am Sylvester. I am the most determined person I've ever known. I didn't want to harass or come off like a creep, so I let some time go by, and then I sent her another message. I do not recall what it said, but it was funny. She finally replied, and it was almost as if we knew each other from another lifetime. We truly clicked instantly. After a few hours, we exchanged numbers and talked on the phone for hours on end. She lived about an hour away from me, but we both had the desire to see each other. So we agreed to meet up thirty minutes away from our respective places of living. Social media helped connect us, because if it wasn't for Facebook, it's possible that we would've never bumped into each other. *Facebook was the soul mate connector.*

We met up for a movie and dinner, and this girl was so beautiful to me. And of course, we matched. Although we didn't plan it, we matched, which was crazy for a first date, and we both laughed at each other's red outfit. We started dating there. I pretty much told her that she was my girlfriend. Although she said no, I still said, "You're my girl." After about a week of telling her that she was my girlfriend, she finally agreed that she was. We hung out every single day for the next five months.

Literally, we went everywhere and did everything together—baseball games, random nights in the city, road trips, breakfast, traveling, and more dates. I can't say that our relationship was perfect, but it was pretty damn efficient. We got along, we talked, and we canceled out the distractions of others. We met at an ironic time because she had just lost her mother and I had just lost my grandmother. She was still healing from wounds from her ex, and I was still not over mine.

Brewing in the background for me was a promotion at my job, because I was literally destroying my sales quotas month after month.

At the time, I was just a sales rep in Illinois, but I wanted to move to management because I am obsessive when it comes to goals and accomplishments. I wanted to lead my own sales team and empower others to be their best. I felt like taking a management position was going to propel me into a position of leadership and empowerment. Ever since I was a kid, all I wanted to do was be a leader and push others to be the best people they could be. At the time, I was unaware that I would find that by being an author. I wanted the promotion to be in Los Angeles, San Diego, or in Phoenix. I wanted to live in the Southwest because I dreamed of waking up next to palm trees and sunshine. I was born and raised in Chicago, which offered the exact opposite climate. It was in late August that the interviews came in, and by early September I had accepted a position in Phoenix.

Dove was indeed not happy about this position change. She did not like that I was moving, and most importantly she did not want me to go, for selfish reasons, but it's understandable. I didn't approach her and tell her that we were moving. I told her that I was moving, and of course after losing her mother, an ex, and now what felt like the guy she was starting to fall for, you can put yourself in her shoes and imagine how she felt. However, I knew that I needed to take the position. I wanted to become a writer and author but felt like I couldn't do it under the pressure and expectations that I had in Chicago. Everyone knew me there for different things, other than being a writer. When I spoke of being a writer, I was mocked and laughed at, literally and figuratively. I ended up making an album before I moved, not because I wanted to be a musician but because the creative arts were a way for me to understand myself.

So I moved. I took the job. I left my family, my girl, and what I had known for a reality that only existed in my mind. My goal at the time was to have the dream job, the dream girl, and the dream lifestyle of freedom and happiness. I was conflicted every single night with this decision because I really loved this woman and wanted to be with her, but at the age of twenty-four, I knew I wouldn't have many more chances to create this dream situation I wanted. I knew that if I didn't leave, it would've been the death of my creativity and my happiness. I wasn't truly happy at this moment—understandably so, as I had just lost my grandmother. I knew I needed to go to Arizona. It felt like the right decision.

Once I got to Arizona, I was by myself, so I dove into my job, and every day I came home and practiced writing. I became obsessive about sales and writing, like I was with football. I talked to my girl every day and every night. I loved her and missed her so much. It destroyed me being away from her, because I wanted her to be the one. I was stuck between the lonely nights, and missing someone I loved, and the confusion of creating a dream life.

Now, this distance brought a new element into our relationship, which wasn't there previously. It brought jealousy and insecurity. These two traits are the most devastating components of a relationship. I believe that any relationship that has jealousy and insecurity will end abruptly. Those are two of the most toxic characteristics that any of us can have.

Time out. I need to connect some dots for you. This chapter is called "Social Media: The Private Investigator, the Problem Creator, and the Soul Mate Connector." Question: How did I meet Dove? I met her because I messaged her on Facebook, and she didn't respond, and so I messaged her again, right? Well, guess what the first problem in our now long-distance relationship became? I'll give you a gift card to Chipotle if you can figure it out. That's right. Our problem became social media and her assumptions of how she thought I was using it. She thought that I was messaging every girl that looked like her, because I message her. This was her logic. This is literally what she said to me.

Let's go deeper and observe this real-life story objectively. What had I done to give her the idea that I was misusing social media? The answer is *everything*. There's two perspectives here that must be noted, and the first is that I found her on social media. I am not naive enough to say that because she is a woman, she never forgot that, but I do know women have this amazing ability to recall things that have little to no value in the present conversation. Again, remember, I'm not attacking anyone. I'm just sharing a very honest male perspective. So of course, she brings up the fact that I was "thirsty" and messaged her twice when she was trying to ignore me. So her perception was that I was doing that since I was away from her. Factually, I was not. I was building a blog, recording YouTube videos, and slaving away at my job. And when I did have free time, I hit the gym five days a week. I didn't go to bars or clubs. I was too focused on building my writing brand and being successful at my corporate job to worry about anything else.

So her insecurities start to kick in six or seven months into the relationship. Today, you may see my social media accounts as beacons of hope or light. You may view them as poetry or thoughts to keep you going. Back when I was dating her, my social media account was a reflection of my job and hobbies of weight lifting and writing, and not really me. I hardly posted images of myself. I just don't have that personality type. I had a Facebook account that was connected to high school and college classmates. Which to me was a normal thing then, but to me now—I don't care what people think about me. I never needed external validation to feel alive or complete. I was always the rogue person who enjoyed solitude and new experiences. To me, as long as you have hobbies and activities, then you will be an efficient partner to date because you will never become codependent upon the other person. And this, my friends, is when the light bulb should go off, because she was codependent and I was not. She was depending on me for her happiness, and once my attention and physical touch were removed, she became an empty shell of the woman I once knew. She went from a fun, confident, and gentle woman to an accusatory, insecure private investigator. She was supposed to be my lover and my soul mate, but instead she acted as if she was confused by her lack of identity. Previously, we had no issues, and then once these elements came into play, the dichotomy of our interactions switched. Our phone conversations soon turned into petty and trivial instigative-style confrontations rather than loving and caring exhibitions of love. But wait. There's much more. The topic is social media here, but you need to know about the next three months in order for this section to really hit home like I want it to.

By the time December came around, I did not want to go back to Chicago, because it was snowing, and it was sixty-five degrees in Phoenix every day. I booked her a flight and told her that she was spending the holidays with me. I flew her out, which I'm sure was hard, because she wasn't with her family, but she loved me, and she needed to be with me anyway. We had an amazing time together, and the timing was impeccable because she had just lost her job back home. The opportunity basically told both of us that she was supposed to move to Arizona and be with me. Look at it objectivity. I had a luxury one-bedroom apartment, a car, and great salary, which I think was $75,000 a year, as a twenty-four-year-old. She had a car with no lease, no bills, and no job. To me, it was the universe telling us that we were supposed to give it a try. I felt like I was a supportive boyfriend because I wanted her to be a food blogger. She cooked so much food and took pictures of everything. Food was her passion. However, I felt like she was wasting her skill by not sharing it, so I told her that I wanted to start a blog and share it. I told her that she could be making six figures or more if she just presented her ideas to the world. I never asked her to work. I only told her to chase her dreams of being a traveler and person who talks about food. She didn't listen to me, obviously, because people don't learn until opportunity passes them. Either way, I ate good, and she cooked every day. I worked and made a lot of money, and we did whatever we wanted to do for a few months, until social media came back into the picture. Again, you need to look at this time line objectively. We were together back in Illinois, and we had no problems, and the distance created our issues. She moved and lived with me, and we had no problems until a few months went by, and the same problem came up.

Someone is going to ask me what I was doing to give her the fuel for her insecurity, and as objectively as possible, all I did was respond to other humans who contacted me or initiated conversations with me. At this point, I had attracted about eighty thousand followers to my blog and twitter accounts, where I shared my words and poetry. This was early 2013. I was doing this only because I wanted to be an author, which she knew and supported until she realized that women read books. Women were the main ones who liked my blog and twitter accounts at the time, which bothered her because her logic was that men should follow me and support me, not women. I remember saying to her, "That is the most illogical statement I've ever heard; women are human, and humans support my writings. The real question is, why don't you?" Actually, she didn't say women. She said, "These hoes love what you write. Why don't you go fuck them?" I can never get those words out of my head. She haunts me still to this day. I was an innocent and naive boy who just wanted to help the world with the art of writing.

Today on social media, I see a lot of jokes about how controlling and jealous women get over social media, and I actually lived that. It's not fun at all. In fact, it's like living in hell because something in the virtual world literally has the ability to ruin your day. I very much enjoy being alive, and the most important thing to me is to have fun. There is nothing fun about being with an insecure woman (or man), but I am a man who writes as an introspective person. For me, there is no relationship if you're trying to fix another person's insecurity. Someone will say that everyone has insecurities, and only a person with insecurities would make such a blanket statement. I do not have any type of insecurity today, and my girlfriend doesn't either. Did I at one point? Yes, I did, but today, which is the most important day, I don't. Insecurities are pathways to destruction when it comes to relationships. Insecurities are not funny; they're nothing to joke about, like how people do online, which is neither cute nor acceptable. It's my number one biggest deal breaker. I refuse to even entertain a woman who is insecure. There's not enough patience or power inside of me to do it, especially when I have dated and been with women who are not insecure. The definition of insecurity is a person who is not confident or assured, who is uncertain and anxious. That emotional standing leaves a person in a place of doubt and shakiness. Insecure people are largely blind and unaware of this; telling them about their insecurities makes their insecurities flare, and they feel attacked.

There's a direct correlation between why Dove was attacking me and her made-up perception of behavior, and it was because of the way she was using social media. She followed the most attractive fitness models, and she spent hours each night scrolling social media, comparing her life to the curated lives of others. She was on my case because one, she wasn't healed from the last relationship with her ex, and two, she was comparing herself to other women online every single day. She also was the typical American girl who idolized and observed celebrity relationships. She talked to me more about what celebrity women in relationships were doing than what we were doing that day. Over time, I noticed that she became obsessed with social media and, more importantly, her perception of how others perceived her and us through the media.

But wait—there's more. She got mad at me because I didn't post about her more often. Now, to know me is to know that I don't care what people think about me and my business. I do not need an outside validation to my personhood, yet somehow I had aligned with a woman who really wanted this type of validation. I hardly posted anything. I feel like I am a good-looking guy, but I don't take selfies often, so why would I post myself? I shared pictures of my food or the sky—those things are much more interesting to me. If you follow me now on social media, you hardly see me. It's just not my personality. I tried to explain this to her but was met with resistance. She flat out told me that I needed to post her so other women would know we were together. My response was, "Humans see us together in public all of the time. You live with me. Who exactly do I have to post this for?" To me, this was a logical question that she had no realistic answer for.

Some of the readers of this book are probably on or have been on either side of this circumstance. My claim is that if you need to post your relationship for others, that means you are insecure. Insecurity cannot be solved via external validation. If the root of your problem is insecurity, how will an external solution solve something that is internal? It's illogical and simply irresponsible for anyone to think that way. If you think that way, please understand that forcing or demanding that another person take pictures of you and share them on a social network to appease others is simply a form of control and manipulation. I have a question for you—do you want to be manipulated by a person who claims to love you? "Manipulation is the skillful handling, controlling or using of something or someone. Whether it's the sculpture you made in art class or how you convinced your friend to do your homework—both are considered manipulation" (Vocabulary.com). I understand that manipulation is a form or power, and power is a normal part of human interaction. But my question to you is, do you want to be that clay sculpture whose only purpose is to be transformed into whatever shape the manipulator forms it into? Yes, of course, relationships change you, and it is important that we all grow, but do you want to be manipulated? Do you want to manipulate people whom you love and care about?

We got into this argument, and she had no logical answers that justified her emotional attack on me. Again, I was with this woman every single day, paid for her life, and didn't party without her. I had no locks on my phone and always included her on extracurricular activities. I gave her no real reason to feel threatened by my actions. Based on the consistency of my actions, she should've been satisfied with me as her mate, but this is just to show you how dangerous and toxic insecurities are.

If you have them, step one is to accept yourself as you are. The main reason you have insecurities is because you compare your body to others. You see your success or lack of success and compare it to others. I am giving the example of a woman who is insecure, but I am not attacking women. This is a specific situation, and insecurity does live inside of some people, man or woman. It's ugly in all of us, and I challenge you to eliminate it from your relationship. No, not your dating relationship— the relationship you have with yourself. It's toxic and does not serve you.

Four tips to erase insecurities:

1. Unfollow anyone on social media who forces you to compare your life to another person. Comparison creates insecurity.
2. Reduce your overall media consumption in half immediately.
3. Work out four days per week; this is the most efficient antidepressant that I have found.
4. Journal. Every day I want you to write about your wins, your journey, and things that motivate you. Psychologically, this is called self-hypnosis, and it will empower you.

She wanted me to post her, and us, and so I did once I felt comfortable and once I liked the photo. Again, it was and still is outside of my relationship to post such photos online. In fact, it is a sign of insecurity actually. In all cases, no, but in some. In this very specific case, it was a sign of insecurity, and I didn't want to support it, because I wanted to work, internally, to fix our problems. However, I figured if I appeased her, it would make her happy, so I posted a photo that I took of her. I never told her that I even took the photo; it was a candid photo of her while we were at lunch. I really liked it, and then she became more upset once she actually saw the picture. She said, "You didn't get the right angle. Delete the picture." My response, word for word, was, "You have to be kidding me, right? I love that picture of you. I am not deleting it. Why does it matter?"

Then she went on to explain why it needed certain lighting and the correct angle for other people to see it and to "like" it. Again, remember that my personality type is to remain private, and I don't care about any external validation at all. This situation was nothing but stress and pain to me, all in the name of making her happy.

First, I did what she wanted, and that was my effort to make her happy. Second, my effort wasn't even good enough for her because I didn't get the right angle. I know there's at least one woman who finds the humor in this because she has done this. Yes, this is funny because it's so petty and childish, but ultimately it's nonsense and a waste of human time. I refuse to label this as a female or male behavior, because I know it can go both ways, but this event occurred in 2013. Three years later, this is considered normal, at least from the observations that I have seen objectively. I see these jokes online, and although I have a sense of humor, I personally don't find the humor in it, because it is literally like living in hell.

The Final Story

Back in 2008 there was a school shooting at Northern Illinois University, where I went to college. Six people were killed that day and twenty-five people were shot that day, and of course, it became national news. I'll never forget this day. The shooter went into the classroom that I had literally just left, Cole Hall, room 101, in the middle of campus. This moment in history was surreal for me, the victims and their families, and the university. I really struggle writing this, but I need you to really understand how impactful this event was at the time and still is to the Northern Illinois University family. The shooting happened at 3:05 p.m., and I had class there, in Cole Hall, room 101, from 2:00 to 2:50 p.m. I literally just walked out of the classroom, and this is something that I am thankful for, but I think about it every day, and I think about the what ifs. I think about the people who were in the room. I think about the shooter. I think about the police who were there by 3:11. I think about how for two weeks we didn't have class, and at that time, there was complete unity among human beings. There were no fights, racism, or sexism after this event. We cared for each other, we hugged, and we went to vigils to pray and hold hands. We cried and lost our egos.

It was a tragedy; it was sad, but there was peace and grace after. This moment in time is one of the defining moments of my life (of many lives), and I hope you are empathetic enough to understand how in 2013 this was a big deal to me. My last semester on campus was fall 2009, so I was only four years removed from the school and five years removed from this event.

I was asleep. All of a sudden, I heard yelling, and Dove was pounding on me to wake up, making comments like, "Who is this bitch Megan?" I was alert, my fight-or-flight mechanism kicked in, and I thought something dangerous was happening. My heart was pounding. I looked around. She was finally becoming clear in my eyes. At first, she was blurry, but now, she was clear. She was upset because of a picture I posted on Instagram. She was upset because a girl named Megan, whom I went to college with, posted the same picture. Yes, she was there when the school shooting happened. Yes, she relocated to and lived in Phoenix like I did. Yes, I knew of her but didn't really know her. No, at that time I did not flirt with or carry on with her on social media or on my phone in any inappropriate manner. Yes, I had to work at 9:00 a.m., and it was 7:00 a.m.

I cannot make this up, but it was Valentine's Day. You have all of the facts, and just like you can't believe this story, I couldn't believe that she was waking me up. Here is the picture in question:

I posted this picture, and based on Dove's rampage, so did this other girl. Please enter my body and be the person lying in the bed. I posted this picture the night before, and I was crucified the next morning for posting this, because the girl that my girl thought I was secretly flirting with posted the same photo. Well, I broke up with her about ten minutes later. I couldn't handle that type of pressure. There is no reason to wake up your lover like that. She made me food after, which I ate, but I still broke up with her. Remember how I told you that she was a really good cook? There was no way that I was going to miss that.

I am the guy who breaks up with girls on Valentine's Day. But I feel like it was an earned breakup, and this is why my claim against insecurity will never change. Insecurity is a path to destruction. It literally killed our relationship. Now that I have healed and grown, I will never deal with a woman who is that insecure. I want to share some poetry from this situation:

Impossible

It's impossible for me to love, in this way, the way that hurts you and me. You project your fear and insecurity on me, as if it's my responsibility to fix you. That is indeed irresponsible and unrealistic. Yes, I love you like the sun's rays that are forever traveling through the galaxy. But I am not as strong as them; my power has limits and eventually fades. I need you to focus on building your confidence and perception. I am your lover, your friend, and I will assist in the best way that I know how, but please remember that all crutches are just temporary fixes until the wounds heal. I am and will be one of your crutches, but, baby, you have to believe that you can overcome. You need the utmost confidence in who you are. I believe in you, now and forever, and don't you ever give up on yourself again. Allow the shadows of your insecurities to fade into the dusk like memories of peers from grade school. Believe, grow, and fight to be the most efficient you.

There is this concept that another person can save you from your despair, and those illusory thoughts keep the user from accumulating the willpower needed to overcome adversity. See, life is truly an amalgamation of complexities and tornadoes. You're allowed to not have it all together, and you should embrace those moments when your back feels like it has been broken by life. These moments create voids and confusion, and that is okay. You weren't created to have answers. At best you were created to have questions, and the most important thing you can do now is seek. Seek new light. Seek new ways. Seek new versions of you, but don't you wait another day. Don't you spend another second waiting for a hero, because you are the one—you are the hero in the fairy tale.

Closure: I did everything I could for her. She had a picture in her head of a picture-perfect man, and it wasn't me. I prayed for her; I meditated with her; I paid for her; I slept only with her. My devotion to her was never broken, but she was committed to her insecurity. The guy before me broke her; she never healed, and I got cut on all the broken pieces. Her insecurity was the Black Plague to our relationship. I changed everything to appease it, but I still wasn't good enough. Her insecurity ran so deep that I started believing the negative things she used to tell me about me. I lost confidence; I became a shadow of the man I used to be. Walking away from her changed my life. She changed what I require from a wife. Once I let go of her, I reevaluated why I had attracted her. Her broken pieces matched mine. Never again will I lay up with an insecure person. That pain is too strange for me. Because of pain, I understand love. My queen has to be a woman of confidence; she has to allow me to help her. She has to believe that I'm the worth-it man, not the perfect man. Experiences like this only make a person stronger and wiser. Hopefully, she grew. I did. I hope and pray that if you're in this position, you grow. There's nothing wrong with being there. However, everything is wrong with staying there. Don't you dare think it is okay to stay in a state of suffering like that. Insecurity is literally the death of a relationship. It's a black hole that destroys everything: you, your lover, and the idea of love. One has to grow, practice self-love, and let go of the past that is haunting you. Continuing an insecurity will push away a good person. Actually, no, let's think about it at a much deeper level than that. Continuing an insecurity will push away the person who is meant to carry the gullies of your soul, the person who will have your back when the rest of the world doesn't. Don't be insecure. Subtract insecurity from your package, and add as much value as you can with these tools: positive self-talk, positive self-hypnosis, physical fitness, and confidence.

Chapter 7

The Dear Queen Concept: Introspection on How To Treat A Woman

My first relationship book, *The Dear Queen Journey: A Path to Self-Love*, was a journey through introspection and self-love. I recall writing the intro, about how important it is for a man to find his queen and how there is nothing more important than that. I still stand behind that. Life is just so much better when you have a woman you love, respect, and care about on your team. Not to say that life isn't worth it if you don't. If you ask any man who has spent time with a woman he loves, he wouldn't exchange that for anything, because he knows how valuable she is to his life experience. This is why guys will pull out all of the stops and tricks when they need to get their girls back. They'll beg. They'll cry. And some guys will even fake suicide. We know that suicide is nothing to joke about, but you and I both know at least one guy who felt like he lost his girl and has said, "Girl, if you don't get back with me, I'm going to kill myself." Again, nothing to joke about, but we know people who have done this, both men and women, who ended up laughing later on about it. I guess that's my way of saying that I did this when I was twenty-two years old and got a kick out of it, in retrospect. That's a manipulation tactic called guilt tripping. Now that you guys have read this book, you're going to be identifying manipulation tactics everywhere you go.

So here's my mission here. I've been very successful with women. Let me explain what I mean, and please accept that I'm saying this based on a guy's value system. Since I was in eighth grade, females have loved me, have loved talking to me, and have always been open and vulnerable with me. I have dated every single race that I can think of. I have dated in multiple regions and different generations. I've dated pretechnology era, while everything was brewing, and now in the full-blown technology era. I've met girlfriends organically by talking to them at a park or in the mall. I've dated online. I've met women on social media. I've been on a blind date. I've been to speed dating. I've met women at the clubs, bars, and nightlife scene. I've met women from the gym. I am a master dater, expert at relationships, and most importantly a guru at understanding women. You probably think I'm a whore. Don't judge me. When I am not in relationships, I try my hardest to stay away from the hook-up culture and the pickup artist life, because it's too easy and way too addictive. I'd much rather be in a relationship, but I don't feel like most women are worth my commitment, so when I'm single, I stay single for a while. I'm just being honest, transparent, and vulnerable. You've read my books; you know that I'm not going to lie to you. I only want to add value to your life, and I know that my honesty is necessary to gain your trust, your open mind, and your attention. I've been toying with the idea of writing a pickup artist book, simply because I have so much real-world experience and education on it. Specifically, the last four years have been spent studying the sociology of genders, the art of seduction, and human psychology, specifically around intimate relationships. I don't have a desire to write a "pickup artist" type of book, because I believe that information can be used for evil, and I would hate for my name to be attached to something like that. I can't control that, obviously. I can only put out good vibrations and hope that people use information to build others up.

But I'll tell you what I can do here. I can take the next two chapters to build a framework, based on gender generalizations, that tell men and women exactly how they push people way. Let's be real—we unknowingly push people away, push people to cheat, and push some people to exude toxic behaviors. Everyone is not secure enough to admit that, but it's the truth. So the this chapter and the next are both for men and women, one focused on the male gender and the other on the female gender. The purpose is to gain perspective of the other side. First, I'll go over the "Dear Queen Concept," which will tell men what to do and what not to do. The second is the "Dear King Concept," which will tell women what to do and what not to do. The information I'm going to share about my personal experience is not a guideline for everyone. It's based on my wide array of experience and education. Take what works for you; disregard what doesn't. I command you to keep an open mind, to introspect, and to share any tips you find with trusted people. I only have two ways to write this. Give you recycled information that these self-proclaimed gurus use over and over, or do it Sylvester's way and give the real, the raw, and the blunt truth. We want the truth and realistic perspective from someone in our generation who looks like us.

In conclusion, some of this can go both ways. Nothing here is solely attached to one gender or the other. If you are a pickup artist and you're just looking for tips, I cannot be mad at you, but I do have a favor to ask. In this book, I have labeled you as a speed dater, the dating archetype that is just looking for fun. There's nothing wrong with that, but all I ask is that you remain honest about your intentions toward the other lovers out here. I'm crafting this book for the lovers, for those that desire to be in or to understand relationships. If that's not you, I just beg that you respect the other person who is sharing his or her benefits with you. This is a disclaimer. The writing style over the next two chapters is very blunt, very straight to the point, and not sugarcoated at all. Don't get offended. You've been warned and have chosen to stay.

Don't Be Too Nice to a Woman—Be Respectful but Have a Backbone

Somebody put this book down after reading this title. First and foremost, do not read those lines and think I'm excusing your bullshit behavior as a man to just treat women however the hell you feel. No, *Dear Love Life* rests on three morals: respect, trust, and communication. You are, at all times, required by me, the text, and your own internal government to respect women. Just don't be too nice. We always hear the saying, "Nice guys finish last." Yes, this is correct. They do. This does not translate into permission to be a jerk or rude or disrespectful. My girlfriend and I were watching a show on Netflix, and it was about relationships. The main couple was having a disagreement. They were arguing about what color carpet they should pick. She wanted green, and he wanted blue. He just submitted and succumbed to her idea, but this was after four or five other submissions. This guy had no backbone at all. She said to him, "You're way too nice. It annoys me." When a woman says this too you, she's emasculating you in her own head. She's lowering her perception of you as a man. This is tough because some personalities just don't really allow for a tough guy to really permeate through. I don't want you to be tough. I want you to have a backbone. I want you to speak with conviction. I want you to be willing to speak up for what you want. If your girl, or any woman, is telling you that you're too nice, odds are you might be missing one of those abilities, or you just haven't expressed it your true self yet. One of the easiest ways to push away a woman is by being too nice. Don't just be a yes man. She wants stimulation and conversation too. No, additional stress or conflict isn't necessary, but if she comes to you for an opinion, a perspective, or thought, have one. **You don't have to agree with your woman to build her up. Have a backbone, and let her know how you feel, what you think, and what your perspective is. Some men think that you have to appease a strong woman and just submit to her will. Yes, compromise, and be like water, but always have a backbone and speak up.**

— *Sylvester McNutt III*

Put a Woman in Her Place with Safety

I'm just going to share a real-life example of what I mean by this. My woman had an issue with me, with the moon cycle, and with her perception of our ability to be together. She was having doubts, which are normal for any new relationship. There are supposed to be doubts because you're turning your keys over to a stranger. She went on and on about how she doesn't know if she can do it, and she mentioned all of these variable that had nothing to do with anything. I listened. I wanted to hear her concerns and her thoughts. I wanted to be in her shoes and really absorb her feelings. I kept saying, "Tell me more, baby." It was genuine I cared. Once she was done venting and getting all of her feelings off of her chest, I took a long, dramatic inhale and exhale. She watched me. I paraphrased and repeated back some of the things she said just like I point out that you should do earlier in this book. I wanted her to know that I was listening. If you want a woman to feel safe with you, show her that you're listening. Show her that her conversation is important to you. As I'm paraphrasing and explaining things to her, I said, "Baby, you need to let all of that go because we can't control the future or the past. All we can do is give our best to each other today. I'm giving you everything that I have, and you're giving me your all. I understand everything that you said, and it registers with me, but it's not all entirely relevant. What matters is that we are going to continue building, growing, and having each other's back. Don't worry about things that we can't control." In my perception, putting a woman in her place simple with safety means that you're bringing her back to reality once mercury retrograde hits. This, when done right, can be seen as a sign of leadership from a man. It can be seen as a ploy to comfort and to reassure her that everything is going to be okay. I will not lie to you guys and act like this is an easy tactic. It took me years to figure out how to do this. Ninety-nine percent of it is in your tone of voice. Always pay attention to your tone of voice.

"If your woman ever starts acting in a way that you would call irrational, extremely emotional, or what we men like to call crazy balance her out with safety. Always let her know that she isn't too much of anything and that everything is going to be okay. Be her safe haven of acceptance, understanding, and compassion. Once she spends time with a man who exhibits those traits daily she will transform. Your understanding of her will make her soul reach a certain calm that she has never felt."

—Sylvester McNutt III

"One of the easiest ways to push your woman away from being your queen is to give the attention that she has earned to another woman that clearly threatens your relationship."

-Sylvester McNutt III

Sexting, Thirsting, and Chasing Attention from Other Women

Fellas, this has to stop, if you're in a committed monogamous relationship.

If you're in a committed relationship, you have to practice self-control. If you're, then what you do does not matter. If you're dating, then it is your goal to explain your dating style to the women or woman involved. I've said it over and over that having attraction to multiple women is male biology and is normal. Any rational-thinking woman will understand that, but why is she expected to understand the unnecessary chasing of sex? It's possible that you and your lover are not having enough sex. Maybe you're too comfortable with each other and are not taking care of each other's sexual desires. It's possible. If she is doing everything in her power to take care of your sexual needs, then you have to stay out of sexually based text message threads. You have to stop chasing other women. Fellas, the attention will always be there. There will always be a lonely girl who is willing to be a side girl while you dip out on your relationship, but that's not what you signed up for. You're a man of substance, so it is your duty to stay committed because the last thing you want is your woman entertaining another man the way you're entertaining these women. Fellas, when you get in a relationship, you become more attractive to other women. They don't care if you have a girl or not. Some are going to think they're better than her, some will play the game to see if they can control you, and some women are just so lonely and horny that they'll take any attention they can get. You will regret it later if you have had access to this book, to these words, to me telling you to stop dealing with the extra women, and then you lose your girl because of your actions. I did it before, and the burn takes a long time to go away. You kick yourself in the ass because you remember saying, "I just need to leave these girls alone and focus on mine." It's never worth it to cheat emotionally, physically, or even innocently. You will push your girl away, corrupt her, and turn her into one of these coldhearted women. Man to man, you don't want those problems. You especially don't want to be with a woman you hurt intentionally, because it's possible that she will never forgive you.

Cut it off today. Stay home.

Focus on yours; build with what you already have.

Stay committed.

She wants a
man
who is going
to protect
her at all
times,
with his
actions and
his words.
She needs to
feel safe,
valued,
and
cherished.

—Sylvester McNutt III

Show Her That She Is Appreciated

This is one of the keys of unlocking the next level of love inside of your woman. Appreciation is what paint, drapes, and decorations are to a home. Appreciation is the foundation of beauty inside of a relationship—the respect, the communication, and the trust are the foundation. After you lay down the bricks of success, then you have to make the relationship cozy, homey, and domestic. Here are a few ways that you can show appreciation to your woman, and you'll have her melting at your every move:

- Write her a love letter. Don't tell me that you can't do it. Just tell me you're willing to do it. That's all she needs. She doesn't need you to be a best-selling author. Just the effort of handcrafting a letter will show her effort that can't be paralleled.
- Go wash her car, or go fix something in her room, closet, or bathroom. This may sound like a huge waste of time, but it shows that you are willing to take care of an area of her life. Trust me. Go wash her car, randomly. It costs about five dollars to go to the car wash. You'll most likely have to get out and vacuum the floor

mats. Now, here's the trick. Don't just return the car with a quarter tank of gas. Put it on full. Yes, she can do it herself. But this isn't about what she can do for herself. It's about putting in effort. I've done this, genuinely, for my woman and will do it again. It works.

- Text her with a purpose: ask her about something specific and not just "how was your day?" If you make your texts about her specific feelings, moods, or occurrences, I'm willing to bet you'll activate those listening skills that we talked about earlier.

- Plan a date that requires both of you to stay disconnected from technology. This is an easy no-brainer. One of the easiest ways to really get to know your woman is to lead her down an environment that will allow you both to fall deep into each other's vibration.

- A woman that is appreciated will always perform better in a relationship versus one that is not appreciated. It is your duty, your goal, and your focus to find out what makes her feel appreciated. As long as you do that, consistently, your woman will dump pounds of love into you.

It is your duty as a man to show your woman appreciation in the way that she needs it. Don't ever have too much pride and think you're too good or too manly to do what she needs. You know, just like I know, that a good woman is going to do everything in her power to uplift her man. With that being said, you have to go all out for her.

—Sylvester McNutt III, *Dear Love Life*, "Appreciation"

How to Love a Woman Correctly

There she is, strong and weak, fragile and tough—so well put together but broken from the pieces of this rigid society. She talks aloud because she wants to express and connect to a deeper level of yearning and feeding. She cuddles and holds you because the warmth of your body tingles her inner workings as she becomes more biochemically connected to the fire inside of you. She is the rain in the middle of the dessert, after dinner during the winter. She's the love letter that goes from a desk in Boston to a pale and dusty envelope that goes thousands of miles. Yes, you're right. She's like the perspiration that occurs on your skin as you walk down Miami Beach in the middle of July. Her presence is a present, and it's omnipresent at all times. So you want to know how to love her correctly? I'll tell you how: listen to the wind as it breaks through the earth's lower-level atmosphere, and it will tell you to hold

her like there is no tomorrow. The w[...]
will push you toward her because her g[...]
are unmatched and undeniable. Take you[...]
hand and palm her ass like it's the last
piece of fruit on earth. Palm her ass in
one hand, grab her by the back of the
neck in the other, and kiss her like the
sun will explode the moment your lips
touch hers. Make her understand that
there is no other option—you are the
lover who will cascade her love across
many generations, planes, and situations.
Erase the doubt from her mind, and hold
on for dear love, because, she is your
Dear Love Life.

ying to build herself up while
ting meaningful and deep
ips around her. Her goals
ding value to other
people's lives because she is a
woman of passion. She's kind; she's
tough, but don't take her for
granted. Nobody is built quite like
her. Her goal is to exude love and to
give it to every human she touches.
She's fragile but she's a rock.
Recognize her ability quickly
because she is the total package;
she's ready to build, to grow, and to
give. She's ready for the long haul
with the right one. If you're blessed
enough to attract her energy, cherish
every inch of her soul, her body, and
her presence.

—Sylvester McNutt III,
Dear Love Life

Never make your
woman compete
with other women
for the spot that
she works for every
single day. Laugh
with your woman
and let her know
that her position
with you is beyond
safe. Make sure
that she knows she
doesn't have to
fight battles alone;
be her place of
safety.

- Sylvester McNutt III

Men Need to Understand Other Men's Value Systems When Interacting with Them

One of my best friends is vastly different than I am. I was having a hard time with telling him information about my relationship because of the way he responded. As a man, there's just a certain level of respect that you need to for another man, especially one you call your friend. It's vital we explore this because as men, this pillar alone can destroy how you treat and view your woman. If you aspire to be a good man, take all of these words in.

Your Boys Are a Mirror—All American men have heard this saying before: bros before hoes. It's another egregious and ridiculous code of ethics that some men live by in this country. It's a slang way to say that the friendships with your guy friends are more important than the relationships with females. This type of saying will get used if a group of guys decide to step out to the club or bar and one starts to straggle away because he started talking to a female. If for some reason the female gives any resistance to him, then another male will say something like, "Fuck that hoe. Let's go, bro." This is tough. As men, we are growing up with this mentality in some circles. It's as if it's okay to push women away because they aren't valuable.

There's nothing wrong with pulling away from your guy friends so you can have a conversation with a woman. The conversation does not have to be sexually charged. Oftentimes guys want to give other guys the pressure of just trying to hook up. Hooking up is okay, understandable, and acceptable based on our understanding of biology. What's not okay is the pressure that some guys have to deal with because of this egregious attitude (bros before hoes). If you want to stray away from the boys to talk to a woman, do it. Don't allow other men to make you feel bad or like you're less than a man because of it. That's silly. Now remember, your boys are a reflection of you; they are a mirror. If they're doing this, it's because you allow it. You have to accept that your guy friends may never change. They may be in their fifties still talking about going to the club to chase women. Always remember that they are a mirror of you, your thoughts, and your actions.

Stop hanging around with men who don't value relationships like you do. As a man, you cannot afford to build a life, aiming to attract a wife, while keeping boys who want to act like boys around you. Be the type of man, and hang out with men, who value treating their woman right, being there for their kids, and who want to be positive contributions to the society.

—Sylvester McNutt III,
"Be the Type of Man"

What to Do When You Don't Align with Chasing Women, but Your Boys Want You to Play the Game—

Fall back. Your only option is to fall back. The male pressure to chase women, to be around a group of women, and to act like how our biology tells us to is not conducive to a man who wants to effectively stay in a committed relationship. I know it's hard to fathom the concept of "not being friends" with your boys, who have been there through thick and thin. I would never suggest that you should severe friendships and burn bridges—no, that's not wise and is not efficient either. I am suggesting that you evolve and fall back from them so you can develop. Earlier we talked about conditioning. As men, we get used to going out and chasing women. It's natural for us. When I'm referring to this behavior, I am thinking of the age group between eighteen and thirty. I am not saying that younger or older men don't do this, but as a group, and pack, it seems like that's the typical age range. So here's the deal. As men, we become conditioned to this behavior. If you already know that you and your boys are going out to the club this weekend, then you are conditioned to it. Not that the club is a bad thing, because it's not, but it's just not efficient to consistently be in the club if you're trying to be in a relationship. That money, time, and effort can be spent impressing your girl or a girl. If you're single and you want to meet women, it makes perfect sense to go to the club, because there are a lot of women in there.

Women dress up, look amazing, and go out wearing the best outfits on the weekends. Typically either they just got paid or they're with their good friends. This is the best time to talk to a woman, because she is in good spirits and is with people she trusts. In fact, I actually believe it is the hardest but most efficient way to talk to a new woman that you don't know—when her friends are around. When I was a pickup artist, I found the most success in the nightclubs using this mentality. Although, in my day cell phones were not a big deal in the club. There were no smartphones, so women weren't on their phones. Now when I go out, I see women constantly on their phones, looking down, avoiding the actual party. Honestly, this is such a strange thing to me. Why do people go out to a party just to be detached and trapped, looking down into their cell phones?

Most women will reject you when they are with their friends, for two reasons—women are on guard, and they'll always look to their friends for signals when they are in packs. If you get the approval, then she's automatically more trusting of you without realizing it, but this rarely happens. Also, women want to be swept off their feet too. I don't believe these women, who are single, that say they don't want guys to come up to them. That's not true at all; they want the right guy to approach them the right way. Fellas, you have to find out what the right way is because all women are different.

Back to the original thought. If you meet a girl in the club, online, or just casually at your gym, at some point you have to recondition your behavior. The next session goes over this in detail. Whenever you reach the point of exhaustion and you no longer want to be on the scene, because you want a queen, you have to speak up and change the mirror. Meaning you have to change who your guy friends are or change how they see you. You'll have to change the environments because the woman you're trying to attract is worth more than the club, right?

The "New Woman in My Life" Prep Mode

The very first thing you have to do is alter the friendship with your boys. This is not a physical change. It's pure psychology. In my writing, I actually use something called causation. It's how I explain logic and scenarios. It's the secret to all of my success. Don't tell anyone. Causation actually gives you the ability to control every situation you get in when opposing logics are at the table. Remember that your boys, who are conditioned to chase women, do not operate at the same frequency that you do. It's possible that you were just out with them last week, but now you're different. You want more. Their logic is valid: go out, get money, and have sex with women. Your logic is valid: I want something different—maybe a commitment, maybe a family. Remember earlier when I had you introspect the concept of truth? Everyone has a different and valid truth. Your truth isn't validated or negated by your boys' truth. In fact, one day he will be where you are, but it's not today. In order to help him understand your logic, you need to use causation. An explanation using this strategy will actually force him to see your logic, and he will leave you alone. Once you express that you're looking for something more, he might give you conflict because that's not what boys do. What you should do is say this, but in your own words: "I'm just at a point where I want more. I want a woman to come home to. One to cook for me, one I can build and grow with. Getting with all these women is great, but I need one I can trust. One that really has my back. I'm going to take a step back from the scene because I'd rather build with her." Or, "If I keep going out and putting myself in these situations, I might lose her. I don't want to hurt her, so I just need to stay in. I'm still a savage, but I'm going to pass tonight." Or, "The last thing I want to do at this point is cause this woman any suffering because I can't control myself. You know how I get at the club, so I need to just pass." As men we understand logic allegedly. By using cause and effect with your boys, you'll actually convince them of your change without them even realizing it. This move is about psychology; psychology is power. Use it wisely. Most don't know psychology.

Delete your exes, late-night creeps, and women who just provide sex. Fellas, we know how it is. We all have that one girl in our phone who will come over whenever we want, and we don't have to give her a relationship commitment. I know, you know, and she knows that you will not commit to her. Why? Because she does not rank high enough on your value-system scale for you to commit, but she is sex worthy. I highly recommend you are honest with women if you just want sex. We can do it emotionless because to some of us, it's just an act. Don't play with this, because a women can and usually does fall in love after sex, especially if she likes a guy. If you have a heart and care, consider cutting her off so she can get a better arrangement elsewhere. Not to say that this arrangement is bad, because some people just enjoy sex. However, this section isn't about her. It's about him. It's vital that you cut this girl off or put her on standby. You have to create an environment for a new woman that is safe for her to bring her emotions to the table. If she comes in and there's eight different women that you're dealing with, it'll be hard for you to choose her, because you have so many options. When you make a decision that you want a new woman in your life who meets your value system, a woman you want to build with, it's imperative that you start to cut the other women off. Some of us have the capability to be friends with an ex, and it you do, be friends with her. That's okay. However, an ex that you can have sex with whenever you want is not efficient. Keeping any woman around that is okay with knowing your girl and still having sex with you on the side has the potential to ruin everything. That girl does not have enough respect for herself to walk away and get a man who actually wants to commit to her. She's okay with getting part-time dick and attention from you, and that woman will ruin your relationship. Trust me—cut her off. You'll prevent heartache and pain later. Fellas, your goal at the beginning is to prove to the new woman that you are trustworthy. All of these women instantly think we are full of shit, and if you're okay with keeping a stable of women on call, then you're proving that. Obviously, it takes time to get to know someone, and that's fair, but you have to prepare for windows of time where you're not having sex or even opportunities to have sex with someone else. When I was younger, I would've never thought about telling other men to create voids of sexual opportunities, because it would have felt like I was telling you to go against biology. I'm telling you to understand that desiring to have sex, as a man, especially a single man, is what you're supposed to do. I am telling you that from an efficiency standpoint, if you want to attract and keep a girl, it's very possible that you have to reduce the amount of risk in your life. In fact, I command you to reduce the risk. How the hell are you supposed to attract, keep, and love a woman correctly with so many outlets to stick your dick in? I'm a man, and I love women just as much as you, but if you want a woman, you have to cut the others off and pick one. In some cases, you have to allow yourself to grow apart from your male friends. It's not that you don't care or love them like you always have. Sometimes you need to create that space so the woman of your dreams can exist in that space. Your life only has so much room between your ambitions, desires, and energy. Always create a lane for your queen so you can stay off of the scene. You have to tell yourself that you're going to choose this same girl over and over and over.

When you really care for a woman, you will find a way to give her the best version of you. Give your woman every part of you: the emotions, the spirit, the mind, and the presence. Every man can experience a better life if he chooses to put the right woman in his corner. Don't waste time, her heart, or your effort. You can and you will find the Queen that you deserve. Be the type of man that will overcome, will take care of home and will lead her to a healthy relationship.

—Sylvester McNutt III, "Be the Type of Man"

Chapter 8

The Dear King Concept:

The Main Reason a Man Will Leave You

or

The Main Reason He Will Commit

This is one of those thoughts and concepts that may be a tough pill to swallow, based on what you already believe. For one moment, please understand that what I'm about to give you is a straight shot, no fluff. My purpose is to help, not hurt, but someone has to be honest with you, and I don't believe in being dishonest with my art.

The common man needs to be respected for the man that he is today. Too many woman in this generation are walking around looking for and expecting perfect men. Women ask me advice every day, and the majority of women who come to me have the most off-the-wall expectations of men that they barely know. Hell, when I was single, I even experienced this too.

Specifically, the first point I want to bring up is how dirty and dangerous emasculation is. To be emasculated, in the literal sense, means to have your penis and testicles removed as a form of punishment. This was a practice in medieval Europe days and obviously is not what I'm literally referring to. Now it is a metaphor and represents the act of making a man feel like he is less than a man. A long time ago, women really weren't allowed to be human beings. Right now, it's a very redemptive moment in time to be a woman because women are encouraged and allowed to express and maneuver through different identities as they find themselves.

Ultimately, the gender roles and expectations of the modern woman has changed in comparison to just forty years ago. Women were told and directed to the path of being a mom and housewife. Again, those are amazing opportunities, and trust me, I am a man who will always seek a woman who takes those roles seriously, because I don't want to raise a family by myself.

Now, what I notice every day is women who make comments like, "I don't need a man" or "A man doesn't complete me." Some women are going so far right now and making statements about how it's more important for them to move up in their careers than it is to create a family. Not right or wrong, but damn, at some point we have to realize that we are being conditioned to be slaves to money and working at jobs that kill our creativity. I've always had the mind-set that your bank account doesn't attend your funeral. In fact, in the last four years I've buried my grandmother and my father, and we didn't talk about their jobs at the funerals. We talked about how they made us feel and the loving memories we had with them while they were alive. So please, logically, help me understand why the conditioning now is "get money and disregard love." Let's talk about emasculation first. I feel that this is one of the most important concepts for any woman to understand. It's one of the main reasons that men leave, men cheat, or never fully give themselves to a relationship.

Ways A Man Becomes Emasculated

Job Identity

Look—I've been a man for a very long time, and one thing I can tell you is that a man identifies with his job. In fact, his job title literally shapes his life. It matters to us. We wan our salary to reward us for our efforts, we want to be known for the quality of our work, and we want to feel like our job makes us 'worthy'.

Have you ever met a man who was in between jobs? He probably appeared to be a wreck and lost. He probably stressed himself out in the quest to find a job. This is because the modern-day man finds peace and identity in his job title. Before I became a well-known author, I was a guy working a middle-level management position with a dream to be a well-known author. But my $80,000-a-year salary was enough for me and her to live comfortably on in my one-bedroom apartment. She didn't work, because she had just lost her job, and I told her to relax and enjoy the time off. Things at work got bad as I started to deal with racism and a lack of support from my management to move into another management role within the company. I let her in on the secret and told her that I was working on my first book. I would write every night and every day at lunch, and she hated it. And I quote, "You can't make a living as a writer." I told her, "You cannot make a living as a writer, but Sylvester doesn't have any options. You're so focused on this bullshit $80K per year when it could be $80K per month."

She said, "Making $80K per month isn't realistic, Sylvester."

Now, what this girl didn't know is that when I was twenty-three years old, in one month I made $17,000, and the way I did it was crazy. I created my own promotion company. I had an online gaming business, did private sales training, and killed my commission at my corporate job that month. I worked about eighty hours each week that month. I was dead to the world, but I made almost $17,000 in four weeks. I kept thinking to myself about how great it would be if I went that hard for myself. Why couldn't I put that effort into my own ideas? I had $75,000 in a 401(k) and $30,000 cash in my checking account. I knew I could just quit my job and make things work out, but no, I listened to a woman who didn't support me. She was fearful of losing this lifestyle she was living, and I was ready to sleep on the floor and not in this luxury apartment, with the two luxury cars we had. I was ready to lose everything in order to create my dream. But we didn't share the same vision. She threatened to leave me if I quit my job. She told me that I wasn't good enough to be a writer full time, and this made me resent her to the utmost degree. I went from loving this woman so dearly to hating her existence. I'm sharing this with you because if you do not support your man and his dreams, it will most likely emasculate him. Remember, your man builds his personal identity around his job. It's important that he enjoys it or at least has your support in what it is. Help him be logical and organized in his attempt to conquer the world. Emasculation leads to resentment, and resentment leads to withdrawal. When a man withdraws without explanation, it is relationship death for the woman, because her intuition kicks in, and she feels the space.

Ignoring or Discrediting His Information, Just for Another Person to Tell You the Same Thing—and Then It Is Okay

This happens all of the time, and the guy just deals with it because he doesn't want to cause a scene. Obviously, now we are slaves to our cell phones that have GPS on them, but back in the day, we only had maps and memories. Remember the television shows where they family would be lost, and the mother would demand that the husband stop and ask for directions? Listen to me, ladies. I know it makes sense for you to ask for direction if you don't know where you're going (let's assume we don't have GPS). We know it is the logical thing to do, but it is also the emasculating thing to do if he has already expressed that he knows the way. If he says, "I have it all under control" or "I got this," what he is really saying is, "Please shut up, and let me figure this out or fuck this up a little but more." He won't say that to you because he loves you, and you're sensitive. So when you ask the strange guy at the gas station for directions, he becomes internally infuriated. What a funny situation. Obviously, we hardly experience that anymore because we have GPS apps, but I think we are all creative enough to understand the situation. Do you get this? I don't need another story, because I think you get this.

Emasculation leads to resentment, and resentment leads to withdrawal. When a man withdraws without explanation, it is relationship death for the woman, because her intuition kicks in, and she feels the space.

—Sylvester McNutt III

Learn to allow your man to fail on his own. With your support, it will empower him. If you nag him and tell him everything he is doing wrong along the way, he will resent you, especially if he actually succeeds in the end.

He doesn't need you to be a voice of reason, because he is exploring, and he knows that failure is possible. He needs to know that you are his guiding light and support—win, lose, or draw.It's about you respecting his process.

Be His Biggest Cheer Leader and Never The Biggest Critic

You actually don't have to support his dreams, you just have to support his efforts towards his dreams. There is a huge difference. It's okay to be an observer and to just allow him to do what he needs to do. Let's be fair. In some cases, you as a woman just aren't in a position to help him with something that he may be trying to create. Especially if he feels like it is deeply connected to his efforts to graduate to a higher level of manhood.

But the second you disrespect or make jokes about what he does is the second he starts to pull away. His biggest indicator of success with you will be if you support him or if you do the opposite: criticize and put him down for things that don't make sense to you. Support him; let him know that he is supported. A man will love you twenty times deeper once he knows that you're his biggest cheerleader.

Also, as men, don't ever feel like you have to push your woman away because of the need to accomplish things on your own. As we mature we naturally realize just how powerful a great partner can be. Your woman can help with you.

Men treat women in a way that is based on this formula: how that individual man views the woman, plus his personal value system and how that woman allows herself to be treated.

—Sylvester McNutt III,
"The Emasculation Concept," *Dear Love Life*

Conclusion on the Awareness of Emasculation

I gave you two examples that are pretty common. As a woman, I just want you to be conscious of how you act around your man. He is fragile. He is a bottle of emotions that hasn't been released. Remember that your man or new man will not know how to express his emotions 100 percent of the time. Let's be realistic—we just aren't trained like that here in this culture. Most men, including me, are trained to suppress our feelings. The things I shared above are emotional pillars of destruction, as far as building a man up. I'm sharing these next few thoughts as a subjective awareness of self. The reason I'm doing that is because if I tell you how I personally feel or have felt, it may help you align with your man. Remember that quotes on the Internet crucify men and make them weak. Most of these writers online like to appease women. Writers in this generation are soft, unrealistic, and aren't willing to be vulnerable. I hope you can tell that my angle as a writer is to share critical thought, awareness, and intellect. I, the writer, Sylvester, will make no apologies for speaking the truth. I will not hold back. I simply do not care about appeasing my female audience. My core principles revolve around being honest, to myself and to my craft, every single day, no matter what. You'll never see me making a public apology.

Let me finish my conclusion. These writers, relationship gurus, and insecure people online are now teaching women that they need to demand a man to be a particular way. They are forcing young men to accept labels that emasculate them, to accept terms like "fuckboy." Look at the way men are portrayed in the media these days. Men are portrayed as abusive, nonemotional, and savages. Yes, some men are those things, but that is a small percent. Men are really getting a bad name right now. I had a show last year and brought up this idea of emasculation, and I was attacked by a very bitter woman. She told me that "a man should be a man and shouldn't act like a boy." I had to tell her how there was no logic behind her statement. Literally, she was showing me how warped and manipulated her mind was. Logically, what is a man, and who is in charge of defining manhood? Realistically, there is no such thing as "fuckboy." There is no such thing as a "grown-up boy."

Beta males are the ones who are creating these illusory, manipulative terms, and their purpose is dollar signs. Trust me. I am a writer, and I have made a lot of money from writing. There are certain terms that we can use that will make us more money. What I'm trying to tell you is that a lot of male writers are beta males, and they are telling women that men should give up their masculinity. These beta-male writers and television programmers are telling women that they need to overpower their men and demand they get treated certain ways. These people don't actually know anything about biology, awareness, personality traits, or gender differences. All they know is that they are insecure and are emasculated themselves, and so they are using these outlets to feel validated. The same version of these men who are giving "advice" are the women who are bitter and entitled. These women are typically alone, upset at an ex, and most importantly, they bash behaviors about men that don't benefit them.

I'm sorry to be "too blunt," but I'm not here for friends. I'm here to be the raw, honest perspective that everyone else is afraid of being. This chapter needed to be written because boys need to be boys. Men need to be respected and cherished as men.

Look—I am a poet and a writer, but I don't sit up writing poetic letters for my female interest every night. In fact, she writes me love letters. If she says something that emasculates me, I stop her on the spot. I tell her right away. I tell her because she needs to know that she's not just going to hurt my feelings, emasculate me, and walk away. That is what real men do. Now, she may not like it, because nobody wants to be called out for her behavior. It's not about allowing her to walk all over me. I am an alpha male. I love and cherish the female energy, but I also know self, and I know that I am not going to allow anyone to walk over me. When you allow women to walk on you, they simply do not respect you, and that to me is the fault of the man for not knowing himself. It's the fault of the marketing, advertising, and writers who are attempting to aid this culture in the quest to emasculate men. It's the fault of women who have not realized how important it is to be women.

Listen to me—as men, we are cowering, and we are scared to stand up to women. We are scared because we are emasculated. We're literally allowing women to be violent toward us, to swear and talk down to us like we are less than them, and for the cherry on top, we have forgotten that manhood, from a biological standpoint, is about leadership. You *can* empower your woman, but you don't have to give all of your power as a man away. If a woman has an issue with you being a man and calling her out, that is her problem to deal with. We teach and accept this idea that "women are always right." It's a joke in society, but you see guys all the time who just submit their desires and say, "Whatever she wants." You don't know self if you just allow this. There is nothing wrong with conflict. Conflict is necessary in relationships. Necessary because it helps us grow. Submission is also necessary. Free speech matters. I'm expressing something real that is plaguing us. If this bothers you, then you may be a part of this community. Speaking up for men doesn't mean you're supporting the men who are looking to put women down. Stop apologizing for being a man. If you're a man, be that. You don't have to prove your manhood to any woman, ever, actually. Just like she doesn't have to prove anything to you. I said in the very beginning of the book that love is about acceptance. Ladies, act like a lady. Fellas, be a man. Do what comes to you naturally, and grow with each other. Stop trying to be what "they" want you to be. Be you.

This chapter isn't for the meek. We are here for introspection and exploration. We aren't here to discuss our biases. We are here to be objective and honest. We are here to be raw and truthful toward our paths. We aren't here to appease our egos and marginalize who we think we are.

In conclusion, if you want to keep your man around physically and emotionally, you just cannot emasculate him. You have to be aware of it when you do, and you have to be accountable for it. You have to understand that emasculation leads to withdrawal. Withdrawal brings a lack of communication, distance, and more misunderstandings.

Four Reasons Why Men Will Not Commit

I present this as an idea, a possibility, and something that requires introspection based on each situation. I've consulted with hundreds of couples and singles over the last few years to establish an understanding of why men are less inclined to commit versus women. At this point, we've talked about biology, evolution, and biochemical responses that men and women have during sex. We accept and understand that men and women are different. I have had an overwhelming amount of women come to me asking why men don't commit. I have to stop the statement there every single time, because that's the victim mind-set. That question doesn't assume any power or responsibility. We've talked about how important it is to be accountable for all of your relationship situations. Millions of men are committed, loyal, and faithful. If you're constantly experiencing a situation where a man won't commit, I'm going to provide you with the five most common reasons. Always assume the power and say,

"Why won't men commit to me?" Yes, that's a tad bit scary to say, but men commit, and if you're having this problem, then you have to be the solution. Be objective and open minded with this information. This will be written solely from the male perspective. This is here so women can use it to their advantage in case they encounter these problems. This section is also here for the men who unconsciously avoid commitment. Here are the top five reasons why men will not commit to a specific situation.

1. He Has No Idea What It Means to Be Committed

This may sound like a no-brainer, but it is not. Being in a relationship takes several sets of skills. If he grew up with a dysfunctional family, with guy friends who objectify women, and with women who only care about status and being loud, what is he supposed to do? Any male who has his face in social media or the media on television can see an abundance of male figures who are glamorized for living the playboy lifestyle. Images matter, so if a young boy only sees the men who brag about getting money, women, and cars, what do you think his value system will be? Also, some men can fully commit to the emotional side of a relationship but not the physical, and for them, based on how their biology tells them to act, this is normal. As a man, it feels unnatural to only have sex with one woman. To have a desire to stop doing that can only occur once he sees more value in being with her versus having multiple women. This has a lot to do with how he was raised, what his experiences are, and, most importantly, what his values are. If you want to be married and monogamous, your goal should be to seek out a man who has those same values. A person's friends, family, and job will say a lot about who they are. Use your discernment here. You can't expect a young guy who is known for having whorish tendencies to settle down with you because you're special. In his mind, he doesn't know how to be committed sexually, because the fast life is easier for him. Some women have to flat out accept that some men are just going to desire multiple partners because they don't know how to be committed. I truly believe that at some point, he will mature and will desire a commitment, but every man doesn't. This is a case-by-case basis. If I were a woman, the most important thing I would look for, if I wanted a relationship, was a man whose morals aligned with mine. I spoke about alignment earlier. You cannot fit a square peg into a round hole. It just won't align correctly. This same idea applies to relationships. Find a man who morally aligns with you before you start throwing around sex and emotions.

2. He Does Not Want to Hurt You, but He Still Likes You

This is a very common situation, and this paragraph may save someone years of confusion, heartbreak, and agony if you listen to me very carefully. If a man says, "I don't want to be with you, but I still like you," don't act like he fucked you over after four months when he has a new girlfriend. If he says that he is not ready to be in a relationship, doesn't want to be tied down, or doesn't have time for it right now, *listen to him*. Do not think that you have the superpower vagina that will trick him into a relationship, just because you like him and because that's what you want. It's such an interesting paradox because you can't trick a man into liking you with more effort. The art of getting a man to want you is solely based on his value system and your ability to seduce him, but it's primarily based on him. If a man tells you that he does not want a committed relationship, listen. It doesn't necessarily mean that he will never want that. For him, deducing that he is ready for a relationship may take you a little bit longer, and that is okay.

However, don't wait years and years for a

man to finally deduce that he is ready. I can't give you a hard number on the expectation of how much time it takes. However, in my personal experience, it has ranged from a few hours to about two weeks to six months. Also, note my age in each situation: a few hours to commit to my high school sweetheart, two weeks to commit to my college sweetheart, and six months to commit to my current girlfriend. I'm sharing this as a possible theory that may help.

Looking back introspectively, the times make sense because there was less risk and fewer variables. My high school girlfriend and I became boyfriend and girlfriend on the day that we met. That never happened again in my personal experience. For me, after her, it took some convincing. We dated for two years until I went away to college; she was a year younger than me. In college, my girlfriend of four years convinced me that we should be together. In fact, when we met, she was dating my teammate, and I actually didn't like her. Her voice bothered me; she annoyed me; she was loud and obnoxious. However, she demanded that I be her friend. I literally remember saying this to her, "Why would I want to be your friend when you bother the fuck out of me?" She laughed and said, "You're going to be my best friend—watch." It took us about fourteen days from that conversation to become committed to each other. With her, I still didn't want to be with her, but she wouldn't leave me alone. She was funny, loving, and caring, and those traits were missing from my life. I really didn't want a relationship, because I wanted to focus on school and football, but a girl like this was too good to pass up. Moving forward to my current girlfriend—I met her last year when I messaged her on Instagram. Instagrammers refer to this as "sliding in the DM." I personally had no idea what was going to happen with her, but here was my logic: she doesn't have that many followers, she's hot, and she lives in Arizona, so let me contact her.

My friends, this is what I'm trying to tell you. Men have different logic for approaching women than women do with us. We don't think about marriage and commitment before we even talk to a woman.

With my current girlfriend, I saw her photo and said, "Damn, this Latina is gorgeous. I need to get her attention." I sent her a DM and she responded, and we texted on Instagram back and forth for about two days before I told her that I wanted to meet her. We met up, and I believe she fell in love with me on the first date. She told me that she was going to marry me, on the first date, but she also said she wasn't looking for a relationship. This type of woman trickery actually made me like her more, but I didn't tell her that. In her case, it took me months to actually decide to commit, because I was dating other women. She knew it. I told her. We communicated. I liked her, but I liked other women too. **I didn't want to be with her, but I still liked her.** In my situation, the reason I didn't want to be with her was because I was unsure of her involvement with her ex and the fact that i was not looking to be in a serious relationship. I didn't know if she went through a healing process with her ex and I wasn't sure If i really wanted to be in a relationship. I didn't want to just be a rebound, and honestly, being a successful, single guy is fun. Dating and not being in a relationship is fun. So why would I want to give that up when I don't even know the girl? I had other options. This is male logic that I'm breaking down for you.

My friends, look at this objectively. Look at the duration it takes for someone to decide if he or she wants to get into a committed relationship. As adults, we all have a process. There's more at stake. There are more variables, like exes, kids, and morals. Again, I liked her, but I didn't want to be with her. The reason I didn't want to be with her is because I had questions that were unresolved, and I never committed to her until I got the answer.

How did I get the answer? Two ways: first, I asked, and second, I deduced the answer internally because I had to accept that she was in front of me—she wasn't in front of her ex. I also had to accept that I'm not in charge of how long it takes her to heal. I can't control that. My feelings for her didn't change. She knew I liked her, but I didn't want to commit until my little mental checklist was completed.

For men, the problem is that sometimes, they are unaware of their checklists that they go to internally, which help them deduce if commitment is right for them. I urge men to do some self-awareness and introspection so they can find out exactly where they stand. The problem comes in once he does not know that he has a checklist, and then you'll waste months and months of your life while he figures it out. Figure out what commitment means to you so you can communicate it consistently and effectively. Also, since you've read this book you fully understand that he may not even know what he wants or needs. Most men will not admit that they don't know where they are inside of their dating lane. One, they don't want to lose the woman and two, they simply don't know.

3. A Man Will Never Fully Commit To a Woman Who Emasculates Him

I saw this video online today. This man was standing in the bathroom. His woman was standing there, and here was her dialogue:

"You've been off of work for ten minutes. It takes you seven minutes to drive home. What the fuck did you do with those other three minutes?" Now, to some, this is funny. I've been that guy. I've dated a controlling, insecure, manipulative woman before. I won't do it for another second of this precious life. Dating that type of woman feels like you're trying to take a bath on the sun. It's a special kind of hell, one that ruins all happiness. I've seen this overbearing archetype woman on more and more media shows and outlets. I have to tell you something. This type of woman is a nightmare to be with. She violates, disturbs, and emasculates him at every breath she takes. This type of woman will attract all of the toxic, negative, and poisonous outcomes we are trying to avoid. There's no way she will get a man to fully commit to her. Why would any man with self-respect want to deal with this type of woman? But here's the kicker. There are some men who are highly entertained by being around this type of woman, and in fact, they won't commit, but they'll stick around. They're a victim of Stockholm's syndrome. They feel bad for, try to save, and try to change this type of woman. Don't save her. Save yourself. Now, this role could be reversed. I'm sure that some of the readers may experience this from a man too, and if that is the case, don't save him either. Save yourself. I've seen an abundance of characters duplicating this archetype online, and it's imperative that we stay away from this. Why? Well first, it's more effective to act like a human being who has respect and concern for others. Second, if you want someone to love you and to be around you, understand and accept that this is much easier when people actually like you. It's so much easier once people are happy around you.

4. He Is Not Ready

I hate when my female clients come to me and tell me that they're dealing with a guy who "is not ready" to be in a relationship. Now, the *only* reason a guy isn't ready is because he flat out uses these words. This is something that runs much deeper than I think anyone cares to know. First, we assume that because we like someone, he or she should like us back. We assume that because we want to be with someone, the feeling is always mutual. He simply may not be ready to commit. That is okay. It's unfair to force someone to be ready when you are. Also note that his uneasiness could have a lot to do with the fact that he doesn't want to commit to you. It doesn't mean he isn't ready in general. This is why you'll see example after example of men who will date but never fully commit, and then they're in relationships a few months later with different girls. It's because whatever you offered him wasn't what he needed to commit, and men have a hard time explaining this for two reasons: one, women are terrible with dealing with rejection, and two, he is most likely getting relationship benefits, and in his mind there is no reason to give up what she is volunteering. That women don't deal with rejection well is a comparative statement based on the fact that men live their entire lives being rejected by women. Women are on a natural defense, so when we get rejected, a mature man will just move on without attaching any emotional assignment to the rejection. Typically, a woman isn't going to show interest unless she feels like it's real to her.

If you're dating a man who isn't ready to commit and you are, your only option is to be transparent and honest. You also have to accept his answer and response. There are only two outcomes: he wants to be with you, just not yet, or he does not want to commit, but he won't mind receiving the benefits you're giving away.

Five Ways to Love Your Man Deeper

1.Let him know what it is you respect about him: He will feel better knowing that you respect him. A man often evaluates love based on the level of respect he has for a woman. The more respect he feels, then the deeper he will love you. This is the number one and most important thing to remember. Men, especially in this culture, have egos that control their human motivations. Sit back and watch how your man will compete with his best friend or brother. This is how men bond and show love to one another. Every man that you will date has an ego. It's your job as a woman to learn how to infiltrate what makes him tick and then support his vanity. So if you're dealing with a man who loves the local baseball team, become a fan. You may hate baseball, but this will make your man love you. Or pick the rival team, and be ready for competitive and aggressive arguments that may actually bring you guys closer. If he teaches, ask him about his lesson plans and the children in his class. If he is a manager at a retail job, do your best to ask him about the crazy customers. Ultimately, once you prod the ego, you open up a channel for him to communicate in a way that he understands.

2. Inform him how much trust you have in him: A woman who reminds her man how much trust she has actually increases trust by doing so. He then wants to bring more to the table. In fact, this is actually a reverse-psychology tactic for him, and for you this is self-hypnosis. No matter what, you actually will develop a deeper sense of trust with him because you're putting those vibrations out into the universe. You're planting seeds that will stay with him. All men are going to deal with temptation, so when a man has heard hundreds of times "I trust you," "I believe in you," or "I love this relationship that we're building. What we have is rare," these statements will always stick with him, so when he has to deal with temptation, he will realize that it's not even worth it. This works in the reverse too. If you always tell a man how much you don't trust or believe in him, he is actually going to have this mind-set: "Well, she doesn't trust me anyway, so I might as well..." You *do not* want a man to have that mind-set. A man with this mind-set will ruin you at every sunset and sunrise. Empower your man with words of power and affirmations of love.

3.Thank him for listening: Most guys hear about how much they don't listen. If you choose to tell him "thank you," he will listen more and get better at it, because he knows it's important to you. Plus, you're rewarding behavior with positive feedback. We spoke on classical conditioning earlier, and this is a perfect example of positive conditioning that will produce the results you want as a woman. In fact, I would do this multiple times a week if I were a woman.

4.Plan and execute a date: The gender role expectation that is commonly accepted is that the man will be setting up the dates. Is this true for all relationships, all of the time? No, we know it's not, but the expectation is there, and in most cases, so is the behavior. If you're in a relationship where you often sit back as your man plans, then you should make a date. These tips are for couples, so if you plan and set up a date when you typically don't, it will only add a new element to the relationship.

5.**Support his strange hobby**: He may be into video games, collecting license plates, or fixing cars that can't be fixed. Honestly, the hobbies he has may not help him build an empire or pay bills, but a man shouldn't be stressed all the time about building. He needs a safe haven away from work and the societal pressures based around being the support.

"Be the type of woman who places her man in a place of care, concern, and love. No other man can compare to your king. Uplift him. Build him up, and make sure he knows that his life is better *with your presence*. Make sure that when he thinks of peace, your face comes up, and always stays there. A woman of passion like you only knows how to love at the deepest level. It's possible that he won't know how to love in the way that you do but the man that's for you will love int he best way that he can. He needs you to activate that. Give him that power. Let him feel the force of your love.'

- *Sylvester McNutt III*

Chapter 9

Efficient Tips for Dating Survival in the Technology Era

Hold on to *any* and *every* genuine person you find. This generation has birthed
people driven by ego, money, and status. As a result, good souls are getting ruined daily. Keep your head up, and be conscious of the energy you give out and connect with.

—Sylvester McNutt, *Dear Love Life*

Over the last ten years, online dating has exploded, and the expansion of the Internet has revolutionized how people in their teens and twenties are expected to date. It's much easier now than it ever was before to find a potential date simply because of the expansion of social media, dating sites, and other connections.

I am still undecided on my personal opinion of online dating, because I feel like it gives people the ability to be lazy and not desire to create relationships naturally. When I say natural, I believe that face-to-face interaction is the most natural way. If you date online I highly recommend that the interactions get switched over to face-to-face as soon as possible, without force of course.

Online dating, however, does have one distinct advantage over IRL (in real life). It allows you to screen people before you ever attempt a face-to-face meeting, The value in online dating that most people appreciate is that it saves time—meaning if my biggest turnoff is girls with green hair, and you have green hair, that lets me know that I will move on and not waste your or my time(just an example).

Here, I am going to list some dos and do nots of online dating. My goal is to provide you some valuable insights on how to achieve your goal. I cannot knock online dating. I've met some pretty valuable women from online interactions.

In my personal experience, I have met women from Facebook or Instagram. I signed up for this dating app called Tinder a few years ago when I was single, but I deleted it after twelve hours. I didn't seem right to me. It seemed more like a hookup site. It did not seem genuine to me. In my honest opinion, there is nothing wrong with dating online via social media or through the dating apps. The most important thing is to never force it, ever. You have to allow conversations to be natural. You'll have to text authentically, and you'll have to put yourself out there. If you honestly cannot find people in the dating pool around you, then leverage social media to make new friends. Have an open mind, and look for events, people who host events, and even just people who share common interests in your neighborhood. I am not closed minded. Yes, I believe that the greatest way to meet someone is to organically meet a person out in the streets, but that opportunity isn't what it used to be. Now, this generation is hell bent on getting to work, to the gym, or to the next appointment. For some, it's not that easy to create conversations with people. A lot of women walk around with their cell phones attached to their face. How is a man supposed to initiate conversation with you when you're trapped into your timeline? It makes sense why people would try online dating, and I am not against it, like

I've mentioned that's how I met my woman. It truly feels like most people are so stuck up their own asses that they don't make space, energy, or effort to actually meet new people. But they post quotes online about how they want love, usually my quotes, but you have to have the behaviors that match the quotes. **Point blank, in order to get love, you have to put yourself out there.** You have to meet strangers. It's how you increase your percentages. So get off of your phone, and get out into the real world.

How to Effectively Date Online

Do Not Lie on your Profile

This is pretty self-explanatory, but if you create a profile that does not reflect your real life, you are only setting yourself up for disappointment. Use social media to your advantage. Take pictures that reflect your life. Go find my personal page on Instagram and you'll see that it is a perfect representation of my life. However, it's still private enough that it is not intrusive. I share food, places I travel to, and different events that I attend. Odds are, nobody is creating or using a social media account because they want to attract Mr. or Mrs. Right, but if you're single, I'm here to tell you that it is possible and no matter what you think we are judged for the things we post. Take away all of the quotes from my page and look at the things I post. The images that are left are mirrors of my real life; this applies to you too. If I were single, I would go look at the women who interact under those posts, and I would talk to them. It's highly likely that a woman who comments under one of my taco posts is a woman I might like but why, well it's because we may share a common interest. This applies to you too. Do not lie on your profile. Keep it consistent with who you are, because you just never know.

Pictures for Women

As a girl, if you have numerous pictures of your booty, cleavage, or bikini pictures up, here is what you are saying to men: "I want to fuck. Message me." Do not be the girl who has those kinds of pictures up, and then your profile says, "Guys, do not message me if you are a creep."

If you're the first girl, what you are displaying and expecting do not align. As a woman, what you have to understand is that due to biology, men are attracted first by the physical. So you must understand that just because a guy finds you attractive and mentions it to you, do not label him as a creep, douche bag, or freak. Granted, there are *tons* of those out there, but most of the guys who are online are pretty genuine.

Ladies, if you have pictures with any guy

on your profile that do not clearly say, "This is my brother" or "This is my father," we will assume that no matter what, you have either had sex with that guy or will soon. In other words, do not put pictures up with other guys in them unless you clarify that this is your friend. In the online space the pictures you put up paint a picture of who you "might be" and if you're trying to date online then being mindful of the images will only help. No, you don't have to say, "This is my friend Tony," but I would make it clear that some people are just friends or business partners, and this person here is my love. Also, I met a girl who was twenty-three, and she left up all of the pictures of her ex. I asked her why she didn't remove the pictures of her ex, and she said, "I'm not deleting a part of my life just for a stranger." There is no right or wrong here, but that isn't effective at all. Guys take pride in who his woman is. Could you imagine me giving you the link to my new girlfriend's profile, and when you get there, all you see are pictures of her ex? For anyone with common sense, you'd say that this is a red flag. It's a red flag. I care about Dove, and want her to have a great life. I don't care about her enough to put her on my social media. She is an ex that I wouldn't speak to if I saw her in real life. I don't care for her so why would I have her on my page? Leaving her on my page tells the new girl that I'm not over her, that I still care about her, and that I still deeply love her. Since that's not the case she doesn't deserve to be on my social accounts. Friends, delete your exes off of their, especially if you guys are not currently friends. In fact, if I didn't use my experience with her for everyone to learn, nobody would ever hear about her. It's not about erasing the past. It's about giving yourself a clean slate. It's about giving your new partner a fair space and opportunity to thrive in and that's more important than your past. This goes for men and women: if you're over your ex, delete the pictures of him or her off of your social media.

Pictures for Men

Every woman has the desire to want a guy who pictures her as the most important woman in the world. Pictures with other women are a big turnoff, but ironically, it makes you more desirable to women. Women say things to themselves like this, "Out all of these women why would he pick me?"

This is one of those double edge swords that I don't have the answer to. You'll have to play around with it and see what works for you.

Some guys enjoy posting celebrity women as their WCW, which stands for Woman Crush Wednesday. Is this a big deal? No. Would I do it? Absolutely not. If she is not my girlfriend or wife, then I have no reason to post her on my account. There are some special cases. I recall a time I posted Serena Williams, and it was right after she won seventeen or eighteen tournaments in a row. She had achieved something spectacular, and I posted it as homage to the greatness of her athletic performance. I believe the most effective thing that you can do as a man is create an environment that doesn't breed insecurity by posting random women. Don't do anything that will make a woman think about you desiring other women. Yes, biology tells you to find many women attractive, and that is okay. Yes, your woman should be secure enough in herself, but you also can help her by not doing things that could add insecurity. There are some guys that won't post their girlfriends or wives, and I don't understand that, because they will post random celebrities.

You fitness junkies are awesome. I appreciate all of you because I am one of you. If you have six pack abs and you want to flash them don't let anyone tell you that you can't, especially a person that hasn't worked for them. However, if you can show your fashion, your outfits, or show your lifestyle I believe that will go a long way. Women do not really want to see only that, although a lot of them will appreciate a man who takes care of himself. Women have a problem with most guys who are cocky and arrogant, but they love men who have confidence. The mirror pics of flexing and posing trigger the cocky viewpoint in her mind, unless you're a boy builder or in the fitness industry. That's different. Use your social media and dating-site profile to show pictures of you with your dog, with your family, or around kids. Make sure your photos are clear and you're smiling. A man who smiles can literally break a woman's barrier down. Dress up nice in your pictures too.

Guys, pictures of yourself slamming shots, hoisting women over your shoulder, or passed out from a night of drinking all need to go. You are not in college anymore, and even if you are in college, you should not be posting these pictures up if you are seeking to attract someone great.

Fellas, I recommend having at least one face shot that has your smile on it. Do not fall victim to the no-smile trend. Smile in your pictures. Women want to be around guys who will make them smile. You want her to smile at your profile.

The First Message

Do not waste people's time by sending "Hi," "Hey," and "What's up" texts or using any type of pet names—these are all turnoffs. What you have to understand is that women get hundreds of messages from guys just like you, so you have to separate yourself. You do not want to be just another "hi" guy.

When you message her, keep it short, but make it unique. If a woman is on an online dating site, then she needs a guy to actually put some effort into her.

Read her profile. See where you connect and if you have any true common interests. If you guys like the same movie, show, or sport, that's a good sign.

The message should contain something you noticed in her profile or maybe the destination scene in her picture. Always make the first message something that she has to explain, but don't make it a boring questions.

Guys, make sure that you instantly show how you add value to her life. If you cannot benefit her, she most likely will not respond.

Here are some absolute no-nos for the first message:

- Do not ask her to meet you anywhere.
- Do not ask for her number.
- Do not ask about something that is explained in her profile. It will just show her you did not read it.
- Do not tell her how attractive she is —she already gets tons of messages about this.

- Do not make any sexual pass at her.
- Do not trick or persuade or convince her that you are anything other than who you exactly are.
- Do not oversell yourself.

With all of this being said, I will leave you with this: be yourself, be original, and be honest. The truth will get you further than a lie will. Remember that your goal is to strike up a conversation so you can obtain an in-real-life girlfriend.

No matter what, go into it looking to build trust, respect, and communication. In fact, I would tell her at some point that you believe those are the most important three factors of a relationship. You've read this whole book, so I'm sure you believe it too.

Ladies, remember that a lot of guys are very genuine—be a little bit kinder to them. A man cannot help his biology and physical attraction. If he brings up how gorgeous you are, don't think he is a pig. That is how men communicate. We want to have an attractive woman. It's the first thing that matters to us.

If you are actively online dating and someone violates some of these rules, or someone resonates with you, please share this text as a placeholder for the online-dating standard.

Good luck, and like I said, "Love is the universe around you if you allow it to be." Your social media and dating-site profiles can connect you to a lover whom you may have never met organically. Don't feel like such sites are not viable places to meet your lover. They are. I met two of my girlfriends through social media. It's not weird. It's okay and is going to be the new norm in the next decade. You might as well adjust now and learn different parts of the game. If you tell anyone in this generation that "we met online," they'll understand. Even the senior citizens understand there is online dating.

Too Busy versus Make Time

Yes, everyone is busy. We have kids, school, and work. I am busy just like you. I get that and accept that. However, going forward, I'll never accept a person who is constantly too busy for me. Humans make time for things they prioritize. It doesn't matter where we are in our interaction, if you want it, you'll make time. No, I don't think people need to be up each other's ass all day, every day, but if you want a friendship or relationship with someone like me, don't ever tell me that you're too busy for me, ever. Make the time, and I will too, and that's a fact. If I'm making time but it's always excuses on your end, don't get mad when I give my space, time, and effort to a person who is willing to do the same for me. We both have to sacrifice and give up time in order to risk gaining each other. Don't be fake busy for love. You'll miss out on the right person and then regret it. Make time, not excuses.

- Sylvester McNutt III

Most Important Message for This Generation

You have an extreme advantage over everyone else in this generation simply by seeing these words. If you can read this, I know something about you. You're authentic; you're passionate; you genuinely care about your generation and the things that are going on. Don't ever say that this generation screwed up. Don't talk about how real love doesn't exist. Don't tell me how people don't care anymore about relationships. You care. You are the source. You are the power. You are the one. You are a bundle of love and joy, and you truly believe that you will attract the love that you claim you deserve. Don't you ever give up hope, because someone is living his or her life just so that person can be with you. Don't walk away and fall back from a relationship just because it's hard. At times, the relationships don't add up. There will be problems, uncertainties, and dynamics that confuse us.

You have a responsibility right now, and I need you to fully accept and understand this. *You* are the most important being in the universe right now. Your spirit, your soul, and your vibration will shift this culture. Yes, you're that powerful, and don't you forget that. Last thing— always remember that life will change; your

Dear Love Life will change. We all talk about wanting consistency, but the only consistency that is promised is change. Don't be rigid. Be willing to adapt, to grow, and to meander through your *Dear Love Life* like a river through Africa. The sun will go down every night, and the moon will replace it. After every dark experience in your love life, you can and will shine again. Never give up hope. Love is the most important element in this universe. Love has the ability to heal, to nurture, and to create in the cosmos. There is no microwave button. You will work at your relationship with yourself, with your lover, and with the divine. Today is the day that your new love life starts. Nothing will ever be the same after reading this. You deserve to be in love forever; you deserve to create that old-school love that's based around commitment, loyalty, and fun. You deserve to be in a relationship that is built on respect, communication, and trust. This is the only relationship that you will create and settle for. You are the source. You are the power. You are the one! What the generation is doing doesn't take away from the fact that you are an epicenter of love, of knowledge, of trust, and of everything that we need. You are the generation. Keep loving; keep shining; keep growing; and keep being the big bright light in the hearts of others.

Be open.
Be love.
Be vulnerable.
Be the one.
Always
Push for efficiency
In terms of dating,
Love, and life.

-Sylvester McNutt III

About the Author

Thank you for reading *Dear Love Life: Efficient Dating in the Technology Era*. I was born in Chicago, Illinois, but I currently live in Scottsdale, Arizona. I am passionate about a few things: experience, writing, yoga, and tacos. I am no expert or guru. I will never accept such titles. I am simply a messenger that has been given a purpose from the divine.

I travel and speak about relationships, self-awareness, and any other topic that the moods in the room allow. If you'd like to contact me personally, would like to book me to speak, or would like to collaborate with me, just contact me.

My e-mail is **slymcnutt@gmail.com**. Please reach out, and I would love to work with you, your school, your organization, or your team.

My Closing Message

What's next? Well, I need your help. I am *nothing* without something that I call *word of mouth*. If you enjoyed this book, I need you tell people about it. I need you to post online about the book. If you look at the front-cover image, you'll see that it's a person holding this book and that she's taking a selfie. Please do that for me. Take a selfie with the book. Post it, share, and tag me so I can see it. Share the book, and give me a positive review if you feel like I earned it. My goal is to reach billions of people with these positive messages. I never want to be famous, but I do want my words to inspire, to help, and to heal millions; I want my words to be known. I can't do this without you. Thank you for investing in the book, and thank you for your support. As an independent author, it's vital that the people who believe in me support and spread the message. Here are my social media links. Please connect with me on *all* of my social media accounts, and let's continue to stay connected as we journey through this chaotic beautiful life.

Connect On Social Media:

Instagram: @sylvestermcnutt

YouTube—www.youtube.com/slymcnutt

Snapchat—@SylvesterMcNutt

Facebook: Sylvester McNutt III

Made in the USA
San Bernardino, CA
03 October 2016